ANGEL FOOD

Cake

ANGEL FOOD

Cake

A 40-Day Devotional
For An Upside/Down World

Bradford Bosworth

XULON PRESS

Xulon Press
2301 Lucien Way #415
Maitland, FL 32751
407.339.4217
www.xulonpress.com

Paperback ISBN-13: 978-1-6628-2855-3
eBook ISBN-13: 978-1-6628-2856-0

About the Cover

THE ANGEL FOOD CAKE cover art was composed and photographed by the author's niece Tracy Bosworth Page at her Atlanta, Georgia studio. Tracy is a well-known highly esteemed portrait photographer. The photo is a miracle in many ways. Tracy's involvement was invaluable not only because of her professional talent and creativity, but also for the bundt pan she provided for the picture. It was originally her grandmother's- the author's mother Jeanne–an Angel to many!

The reader might wonder, *What in the world is the purpose of all those other objects and figures in the picture?* Keep reading with this devotional and you are bound to see they are not there by coincidence.

Dedication

THIS BOOK OF MEDITATIONS IS DEDICATED to the women in my life. To women who have been and passed; who have shared love and intimacy with me but have moved on and are no longer a part of my life; and who are here with me now. All, I am convinced, were put in my path by our Creator to teach me to learn in love. I have grown and am growing because of these women. You all know who you are. Thank you.

I will name just a few: my mom, Jeanne; Aunt Betty; Momma Francis; Donna; Sandra; Becky, the mother of my two amazingly beautiful daughters, Maggie and Jeanne; and my wife, Patti, a strong tower of faith.

I would not be who I am without the role all these ladies played in my life, and for that I am eternally grateful!

Acknowledgements

Even though I have been writing most of my adult life, I never really believed in myself as a legitimate and talented author until 2013 when my work was first published in "Alive Now", a periodical published by Upper Room Books. Subsequently, I was published for three consecutive years as a contributing writer in their 365-day devotional book titled *Disciplines*. In addition to the editors at the Upper Room, I want to thank Reverends Barbara and Joey Hatchel for encouraging and vetting my sample submission for *Disciplines* as well as the first draft of *Angel Food Cake*. I am grateful also to Reverend Whit Martin and Reverend Mack Riley for critiquing my annual contributions to *Disciplines*. The willing support of all these pastors gave me the impetus to create *Angel Food Cake*.

TABLE OF CONTENTS

INTRODUCTION

⟋⟍⟋⟍

THERE IS A LITANY OF KEY BIBLICAL FIGURES in the story of God who have taken the journey of self-reflection through forty days and forty nights, either into the wilderness or to the top of the mountain. In fact, the first reference is immediately illustrated with Noah and the great flood (Genesis 7:4). This story of the Ark is soon followed in the famous second book (Exodus 24:18), when Moses goes to the mountaintop and comes back after another forty-and-forty with the Ten Commandments. Because Moses loses his temper with the people of Israel and breaks the tablets, he must return for the second edition of the great law (Deuteronomy 10:4).

Angel Food Cake derives its name and devotional inspiration not from these two earliest leaders and their stories, but from two most influential personalities, Elijah and Jesus, found in later, similar examples in the Word of God (1 Kings 19:8 and Matthew 4:2). These two excursions are for entirely different reasons; one prompted by fear, the next by love. The two provide a nice bridge between the Old Testament's stark warnings and the New Testament's good news!

Angel Food Cake, in fact, draws its name from Elijah's experience in 1 Kings 19: 4-9 (NKJV):

But he himself went a day's journey into the wilderness and came and sat down under a broom tree. And he prayed that he might die, and said, "It is enough! Now, Lord, take my life, for I am no better than my fathers!"

Then as he lay and slept under a broom tree, suddenly an angel touched him and said to him, "Arise and eat." Then he looked, and there by his head was a cake baked on coals, and a jar of water. So, he ate and drank, and lay down again. And the angel of the Lord came back the second time, and touched him and said, "Arise and eat, because the journey is too great for you." So he arose, and ate and drank; and he went in the strength of that food forty days and forty nights as far as Horeb, the mountain of God.

Elijah was no shrinking violet. Just prior to this experience he had approached the dark ruler, Ahab, and confronted him about the business of worshiping false idols. Elijah was a passionate man; zealous for the Lord, and a most respected and revered Hebrew leader and prophet. However, a powerfully seductive woman named Jezebel made him run for his life. Just when he was ready to give it all up, he fell asleep under that broom tree.

How many times have we been ready to give up, losing faith that our good Father will provide for us? How is it that a man such as Elijah — one who called down fire from the Lord to the sacrificial altar of Baal, a messenger to whom God had revealed so much, a bold and brave man who had declared draught and famine on the people of Israel — could be so fearful that he would have to run for his life and ask of the Lord, *"Take my life"*?

Although a heralded man of God and a bold prophet for Yahweh's chosen people, Elijah was just like us and as we are — human. We all have days, periods in our lives, where we figuratively drive off the pavement onto the soft shoulders that warn us of an impending ditch. We have diverted our attention, our hopes and our desires away from our Creator and onto the many distractions (false idols) of the world. This is especially disconcerting when we have already been to the mountaintop, the place of peace where our connection with our heavenly Father is one of a sharp and clear channel.

This forty-day devotional is intended as a spiritual method to help regain our connection with the Creator of the Universe. The writer himself was feeling wheels on gravel, not even hearing a voice through the static, when he decided to compose this book. The initial formation, including this introduction, were put to paper during his personal forty-day abstinence from social media and television in the home. It is likely important for us to eschew something from our everyday routine; most especially things (false idols) of the world that give us diversionary delights.

Angel Food Cake marks it starting point on a Wednesday (Day 1). This meditational tool can be used as a Lenten season overlay. The seven Sundays, when the Church gathers for worship in fellowship, are considered festival days and they are not counted for the forty fasting days. The writer suggests the reader(s) can use this devotional in the same way in other seasons of the year. We can never know when we will fall away from Yahweh and lose our connection with our Creator. We might miss the mark at any time, and we will be grateful to know we have methods at our fingertips that will help us turn back toward the certainty of Immanuel. Except for "First Steps Sunday", there will be no devotions on Sundays. Instead, study questions are included for Sunday School/small group discussion.

Frequently, our need for reconnecting with Yahweh can be surprisingly pronounced in times of great prosperity when we awaken victoriously on the figurative mountaintop. Success and good fortune can be just as treacherous to our spiritual health as when suddenly we find ourselves wandering, lost in the wilderness areas of everyday life. Hopefully, *Angel Food Cake* can be your go-to lift when you find yourself in either of these two places.

ESCHEWAL

*For the grace of God has appeared that offers salvation to
all people. It teaches us to say "No" to ungodliness and
worldly passions, and to live self-controlled, upright and
godly lives in this present age…*
– Titus 2:11-12 (**NIV**)

WHAT IS THE PRIORITY OF OUR LIVES? ARE
we even aware of what our priorities are? How do we
spend our time daily? How do we allocate our resources? By
striving to answer these questions we might identify what
objects, activities or pastimes attract our attention or "idol
worship". In many cases these activities, objects of our attention, create for us diversionary pleasures (lusts). Some are
already identified by our culture's norms as unhealthy, either
physically, psychologically or both; for example, abuse of
alcohol, drugs, and pornography. Then there are those pur-
suits that may be engrained in society as acceptable or even
necessary on which we become dependent like gambling,
viewing television, social media interaction, video gaming,
or even surfing the internet. Have you ever forgotten and
left your cell phone somewhere and felt a sense of panic?

As the apostle Paul pointed out in his mentoring letter
to Titus, these are our "worldly passions". To the extent
that we allow these activities to take priority in our lives,

we create separation from God and there is static instead of conscious contact with our Creator. Take some meditative time to discern what "worldly passion" you might eschew during this forty-day devotional exercise.

Write your fasting ideas here:

Chapter I

Beginnings

First Steps

EVERYTHING IS NEW TODAY! GOD'S WILL IS for us to become learned again and again. Our journey to heaven must be taken up once more with effort. With our Creator's help, the effort takes on divine diligence. We want to live life in grace, for living in grace brings us about as close to heaven as we can be here on earth. Jesus is our model for this effort.

Let us look up with searching eyes for our good Father, craving pure spiritual milk like newborn infants (1 Peter 2:2). Let us wait if we can't find Him at first, being quiet and still. Maybe we are disoriented today, straying from our route with no compass to direct us. We should call out for the Good Shepherd, speak His name. Surely, He will hear our pleading, bleating and come again for us as He always has and will do today and forevermore.

Assuredly we will hear His voice, for the sound of it comes from within, carried on the wings of the Holy Spirit. It will lift us up off our hands and knees. Our hands stretch out, reaching for His touch, and our awkward steps become steadier as He takes our hand to lead us home once more to a place where there is an aroma of love. Together, let us taste and see once again that the Lord is good! Amen.

TOUCH OF CREATION

*I will stand at my watch and station myself on the
ramparts; I will look to see what he will say to me, and
what answer I am to give to this complaint. Then the Lord
replied: "Write down the revelation and make it plain on
tablets so that a herald may run with it. For the revelation
awaits an appointed time; it speaks of the end and will not
prove false. Though it linger, wait for it; it will certainly
come and will not delay.*
– Habakkuk 2:1-3

I T IS EASY FOR ONE TO SKIP OVER THE BOOK
of this prophet whose name is unfamiliar and hard to
pronounce. But Habakkuk, lamenting of his Creator's
seeming indifference to the people's hardships, was a man
trying to have a conversation with his God. He learns that
God often must reach out and twist our ear, grab us by the
collar and shake us out of our slumber. He touches us where
we are soft or hard hearted.

For this writer, although his composition ends up in
a digitized Word file finished off on a computer screen, it
always includes the action of pen to paper in its genesis. The
creation would not be complete in its evolution without the
holding of the writing utensil. The work never arrives on
time whole, its soul intact, where the pen touching paper
has not played a pivotal role in its inception.

And so it is with us. We were meant to be in fellowship. The pen's purpose is not met without a paper partner. "Where two or three are gathered..." (Matthew 18:20). To be God's writing instrument, leaving our mark on this world, we need touch. Were we to hold and be held, if only once weeping in someone's arms, then we are to experience God's eternal love for us. We are His children.

Oh, how valuable it is, the touch of the page. Have you ever sat with a book open on your lap and been moved to the point of running your fingertips across the page and then pausing? We take a deep breath while reaching for the corner, and then we turn the page. It is a new day now, and we pick up our pen again. What will God have us write today, in this world?

The hand-written note is a lost art nowadays. How many people ever have the experience of opening a hand-written card or letter? In today's social media world of faux fellowships, we can touch someone's soul by picking up the pen and signing by our names – *Love, Brad...xx...oo!*

Father, may we always be reaching for Your touch that lifts us into your Grace embrace. Amen

WAKE UP CALL

And all these blessings shall come upon you and overtake you,
because you obey the voice of the Lord your God:
— Deuteronomy 28:2 (NKJV)

I LIVE IN A SMALL HOUSE ALMOST ON THE crest of a hill, a stone's throw from Dobbins Air Reserve Base, Georgia and often in the morning I can hear "Reveille" broadcasting over the Base public address system. I recognize this music and have an idea of what the Base personnel's response to it is. I also know that it is morning and, for those not so already, it is time to rise; time to obey the call! It is the official start of the busy day, a patterned routine to follow as if by script. I can relate to that bugle call and have empathy for the hearers' emotions, for I was once a cadet at a military boarding school for four years. Today I can set my clocks by the notes rushing through the windows, for it resounds at 8:00 am every morning.

The Lord our God is here with us each morning and every moment of the day. Oh, were we to hear His voice and recognize it so definitively, surely the blessings would come. We know this to be true for we have heard His voice at times, and we have received His grace. The French origin of this word, *reveille*, means to awaken (Merriam-Webster, 2021), and like the trumpeter's tune, our Father's voice allows us to awaken to His will for us when we hear it.

During the summers and winters when the windows are closed, and heating and air-conditioning are at work, I go long periods of time without hearing this daily clarion call, and I realize I have missed its familiar beckoning. Even during spring and fall when the windows are open, the music may be faint or strong depending how the wind blows. And so it is for me. When I wander from God or when I am following the worldly winds, I cannot hear the voice of the Lord clearly and I begin to get sleepy again and again.

Abba, may we begin each day seeking Your guidance and open the windows of our souls to Your awakening voice in joyful obedience. Amen.

SIGHT LINES

Why do you look at the speck of sawdust in your brother's
eye and pay no attention to the plank in your own eye?
– Luke 6:41

T HERE IS A GROUP OF MEN WHO MEET EVERY
Monday; a support group that numbers around thirty
on most nights. We are all broken and have a common
affliction. We meet to share our experience, strength, and
hope with each other. When I started attending this group
that we call "Sons of Serenity," there was another younger
man who was a regular there. I could see that he was well
accepted, part of an "inner circle," so to speak, of the regular attendees. I noticed some things about this young man
that were annoying to me. Perhaps it was some of the things
he shared or the way he spoke. I thought he was phony in
what he portrayed. Fortunately, the group was stronger than
the individual (me), and I did not act upon my feelings nor
take them to heart.

About five months later, I remember walking into the
meeting and seeing the aforementioned young man and
thinking to myself: *Why, how remarkable it is that he has
changed so*. He was not the same guy! My cold disdain had
been replaced by warm admiration. Soon thereafter, I saw
him at a public concert I was attending with my family, and
I was so eager to introduce them to this young man when
we crossed paths.

Soon the epiphany came: It was not this young man who had changed, but I. All the things I had been critical of in this person were characteristics of myself that I did not like. Because of a disciplined program of self-evaluation and willingness to see my part in all situations, I could grow. I became able to remove the plank from my own eye and to love this neighbor as I loved myself.

A few years later I was visiting another group; this time of men and women. I heard an older gentleman share, "If you spot it, you got it!" It is just as Jesus' words were in his great sermon.

Yahweh, grant that we would always look inside ourselves first to learn how we may grow in Your love. Amen.

FRAGRANCE OF ANGELS

*But thanks be to God, who always leads us as captives
in Christ's triumphal procession and uses us to spread the
aroma of the knowledge of him everywhere. For we are
to God the pleasing aroma of Christ among those who are
being saved and those who are perishing.*
– 2 Corinthians 2:14-15

WALK INTO AN AGING ROOM AT A DIS-
tillery or winery and you will likely experience a per-
vasive, yet subtle, aroma of the liquid resting in the many
barrels stacked to the ceiling. The smells will be familiar,
but not exactly distinguishable. In the nose, you might recognize some flavor components of the whiskies or wines
residing in their temporary barrel homes; like rock candy,
green apple or black cherry. Visitors might also detect
nuances of the wooden staves which have also been known
to impart vanilla into some spirits. Of course the key component, alcohol by-product itself, will have neither flavor
nor aroma. Over the course of the maturing process, a small
amount of these destined-for-market beverages will vanish
literally into thin air, never to flow across the taste buds of
the thirsty, consuming populace. Instead, those vanishing
traces remain only as aromatic evidence. Industry families
and cellar masters around the world refer to this common
and familiar fragrance as the "angels' share".

For two decades, I worked in the distribution/retail chain of the beverage alcohol industry. As I stood in these rooms, I experienced God's palpable presence there and the "angels' share" carried true meaning. Consider the stages of creation that have taken place for the precious juice to reach this point in its evolution. We witness what centuries of finely-honed craftsman skill have wrought. These simple gifts from our Father's creation make our lives here so wonderfully blessed and enjoyable. Many might think that the alcohol contained in these beverages is the primary component. Not so; it is the water moving from root (quenching the thirst of the vine) to branch, facilitating the maturing of the fruit. The same water that nourishes the grain and prompts seed germination cradles the pomace and mash in the fermentation stage. In the same way, the Living Water from Jacob's Well within us, as maturing fruit, brings the fragrance of Christ as "angels' share" to the world.

Abba, we long to be messengers, releasing the scent of Your Son into the world. Amen.

Psalm 34

I will extol the Lord at all times;
his praise will always be on my lips.
I will glory in the Lord;
let the afflicted hear and rejoice.
Glorify the Lord with me;
let us exalt his name together.
I sought the Lord, and he answered me;
he delivered me from all my fears.
Those who look to him are radiant;
their faces are never covered with shame.
This poor man called, and the Lord heard him;
he saved him out of all his troubles.
The angel of the Lord encamps around those who fear him,
and he delivers them.
Taste and see that the Lord is good;
blessed is the one who takes refuge in him.
Fear the Lord, you his holy people,
for those who fear him lack nothing.
The lions may grow weak and hungry,
but those who seek the Lord lack no good thing.
Come, my children, listen to me;
I will teach you the fear of the Lord.
Whoever of you loves life
and desires to see many good days,
keep your tongue from evil
and your lips from telling lies.

Turn from evil and do good;
seek peace and pursue it.
The eyes of the Lord are on the righteous,
and his ears are attentive to their cry;
but the face of the Lord is against those who do evil,
to blot out their name from the earth.
The righteous cry out, and the Lord hears them;
he delivers them from all their troubles.
The Lord is close to the brokenhearted
and saves those who are crushed in spirit.
The righteous person may have many troubles,
but the Lord delivers him from them all;
he protects all his bones,
not one of them will be broken.
Evil will slay the wicked;
the foes of the righteous will be condemned.
The Lord will rescue his servants;
no one who takes refuge in him will be condemned.

Appetite for the Truth

O N THIS FIRST OF SEVEN SABBATHS, WE complete our *First Steps* of this 40-day devotional journey. Our scripture for today could have applied to most of our previous *First Step* devotions as witnessed in the following verses: *"The afflicted hear..." (2); "...He heard me,"* *(4);" Keep your tongue from evil," (13); "The eyes of the Lord are on the righteous, and His ears are attentive to their cry"* *(15).* However, we will focus on perhaps the most familiar – *"Taste and see that the Lord is good" (8)* — as our theme focus today. It is fitting that we should wade into the entire

34th psalm. It is a psalm for the senses. *"Glorify the Lord with me; let us exalt His name forever (v.3).*

When I catch a cold, have head congestion and a stuffed up nose, my taste buds don't work correctly and food does not taste as it should. Have you ever had to swallow castor oil? As a kid, I would have to hold my nose to be able to get a teaspoonful down. If something does not have a pleasing aroma, we usually do not want it to touch our tongue. We do not have the taste for it. As our faith and our relationship with the Father are growing, we lose our taste for unseemly behavior, activities and programming. So it is that the more our senses are tuned into our Creator's will for us, the more distaste we will have for that which defiles us, as described in Mark 7:20-22.

Our sweet solution is found in the truth manifested and embodied in Jesus, the Christ. Once we have tasted of the truth, we can surely see that the Lord is good! We will know we are free, not dependent on, nor needing the diversions of worldly pleasures. It is just as the Wonderful Counselor told us in John 8:31-32: "To the Jews who had believed him, Jesus said, 'If you hold to my teaching, you are really my disciples. Then you will know the truth, and the truth will set you free.'"

Yahweh, may You forever remind us to hold tight to Your precious Son's teachings, creating a ravenous appetite for that which sets us free! Amen.

Festival Day — Discernment

When are we ready to take off our training wheels and rid ourselves of them? How does the Father touch us to let us know it is time and we are ready to carry the message?

What practices can we start now that will allow us to more clearly hear what God is trying to say to us? What allows us to open the windows of our souls?

Do we belong to an accountability support group? How often do we attend? Does this group represent an integral component in our faith walk? Are we being honest with ourselves?

Introduce a new scented candle or incense to your daily quiet prayer and meditation time. Ask yourself, "In how many ways can I experience the fragrance of God's love for me?"

We should identify those activities, habits, and behaviors that we no longer practice, exhibit, or possess because they are distasteful to us now. Which ones lose their appeal, their *taste,* as we mature spiritually?

Pray Psalm 34 in solitude, as a couple, or as a group.

Chapter II

Transition

"Come back to your senses as you ought, and stop sinning…"
– 1 Corinthians 15:34

*A*NGEL *FOOD* C*AKE* IS MEDITATION FOR THE senses. You might have noticed this in Chapter I. It is when we are quietly still that we can approach the present moment and situate ourselves in the now. Now is all that matters. To arrive in the *now*, we are either transitioning from the past (where all our guilt and shame reside) or the future (where we most oftentimes experience fear and worry). Position yourself in a comfortable place and, for the next five weeks, together we will come to our senses.

Suggestion: Use your open *Holy Bible* and read all scripture prior to each devotion. Meditate on it. Each daily devotion is followed, concluded with a prayer. Try speaking or whispering it to Yahweh. Enjoy!

Taste

SALT OF THE SOUTH

You are the salt of the earth. But if the salt loses its saltiness,
how can it be made salty again? It is no longer good for
anything, except to be thrown out and trampled underfoot.
– Matthew 5:13

A WOMAN I AM CLOSE TO SPEAKS OFTEN OF a man very influential in her life. This man was the model who defined a godly man for her. Bob, as he was known, was a good neighbor, loyal and dedicated to the company who employed him, and a faithful deacon in his little country church. Most importantly, he was a devoted father to his two impressionable daughters. My friend, who is one of the daughters, remembers that her father stopped on the way to church every Sunday morning to pick up a broken man and take him to God's house. It seems the broken man, a doctor, had lost his driving rights because of a weakness for the bottle. No matter, because this man had a friend who was in Christ Jesus.

I have been trying to remember the first time ever I heard one person describe another as, "salt of the earth." I want to believe I heard it first in my high school years in the Deep South of Chattanooga, Tennessee. Over the years, I have understood the phrase to characterize a man of credible character. There is no question it is resultant of Jesus's Sermon on the Mount as documented in the Gospel of Matthew. Records show it was first published in the fourteenth century as an idiom of character reference in Chaucer's "Summoner's Tale". Of one thing I am certain: The characterization engendered in me a feeling of respect and admiration before I was ever aware of its original source. The truth always resonates in us because it is written on our hearts by God when we are created.

Although I never met my friend's dad he was, by chance, also a son of the Deep South. Although she was born in Texas, the daughter's story took place in Memphis, Tennessee. Perhaps this story's doctor had lost his salt and been trampled underfoot. No matter, because he found saltiness in a servant of the Lord, Bob Young, "the salt of the earth."

Father, may we bring the flavor of Christ to all those in the world who have been trampled underfoot. Amen.

EAR BUDS

How sweet are your words to my taste,
sweeter than honey to my mouth!
– Psalm 119:103

HERE WE HAVE ONE OF THE WONDROUS mysteries of our Father's creation. Spoken words we hear are processed and translated as though we tasted them. How is it our sense of taste can be affected through listening? The love of Christ, as expressed in the unmerited grace of God, is multi-faceted like a precious gemstone. Each time we experience its beauty from a different, sparkling angle, it is a facet anew. Our desire is to witness to the experience, as the psalmist sings, "Sweeter than honey to my mouth."

I was having lunch with my longtime and authentically good friend, Louie. We were brainstorming how I might write new marketing material for his emerging line of Bloody Mary mixes. I was already in wonder of his late-life success with his Papa Lou's brand. I had worked many years in the beverage distribution business with this distinctly original bartender, who sported a trademark handlebar mustache. Now, each bottle of Papa Lou's mix proudly displays his greying visage.

Our young waitress, a bartender on weekends, shot my friend some sideward glances as though she had seen him somewhere before. Papa Lou began a veiled and brief survey about his products without mentioning his name. He asked how they had been received by customers. Her widening smile and profuse accolades towards the mixes gave away her recognition. I thought I was having lunch with a rock star! As I observed Louie's demure acceptance, a sweet wave of uplifting grace poured over the moment with every flowing word of the young girl's praise. Papa Lou was being blessed for creating a substance that brings flavor to life, a purpose not unlike the one our Father has set for His children. My friend's passionate love for the beverage of fellowship inspired his fulfilling purpose. After all, what are we here in this world for, but to provide delectable content? It's a beautiful thing.

Yahweh, may the works of our hands and words of our mouth be always pleasant in Your sight. Amen.

SWEET MILK OF SALVATION

Like newborn babies, crave pure spiritual milk,
so that by it you may grow up in your salvation, now that
you have tasted that the Lord is good.
– 1 Peter 2:2-3

MY FIRST BIG GULP OF PURE, SPIRITUAL milk came when I was a pilgrim on the Men's North Georgia Walk to Emmaus #144. The Walk to Emmaus is a three-day Christian retreat where worship, fellowship, and Holy Communion are sprinkled atop a short course in Christianity. The Emmaus community — male and female — is ecumenical, designed to nurture leadership in today's Church, the body of Christ. Mine was a profound, spiritual experience where I learned firsthand the meaning of, *"On earth as it is in heaven."* The experience turbo-charged my faith walk and for most of the past decade I have fully engaged myself in our North Georgia Emmaus community.

For me, the Christian faith is a measured, steady growth curve influenced by disciplined prayer and meditation, peppered with service and a reflective, daily personal inventory. I was an infant in the faith when I went on that 2010 Walk as a pilgrim. As my relationship with Abba grows and my faith matures, I am beginning to see more clearly. Nevertheless, I still crave that pure spiritual milk, for I am prone to self-deprecation! Often, salvation appears fleeting and distant, so I yearn to serve on Walk to

Emmaus weekends. On every occasion, the experience helps me grow in my salvation.

In October 2011 after a prolonged illness, my older brother Marty passed away days before a Walk on which I was scheduled to serve. With no funeral arrangement conflicts, my family urged me to continue in service. I arrived late after team commissioning. One of our Spirituals (pastors) summoned me aside to serve me Holy Communion and proceeded to tell me that the entire team had just been in prayer for me and my family! I remember it as clearly as if it were yesterday. In that moment, I grew a little in my salvation and indeed tasted that the Lord is good.

Yahweh, may we learn a little each day how to cut ourselves some slack so we might grow a bit more in the salvation of Your precious Son. Amen.

THE FALLING AWAY

*It is impossible for those who have once been enlightened, who
have tasted the heavenly gift, who have shared in the Holy Spirit,
who have tasted the goodness of the word of God and the powers
of the coming age and who have fallen away, to be brought back
to repentance. To their loss they are crucifying the Son of God all
over again and subjecting him to public disgrace.*
– Hebrews 6:4-6

IN THE ROOMS OF ALCOHOLICS ANONYMOUS
the words are spoken, "I am either getting closer to or
further away from my next drink." In the *Big Book* of AA,
on page 85, one will find this statement: "What we have
is a daily reprieve contingent on the maintenance of our
spiritual condition" (Anonymous Press Study Edition of
Alcoholics Anonymous, 2008). It is from the chapter titled
"Into Action". Our Hebrews author directed a similar message to Rome's Jewish Christians who were falling away
from the Gospel. These new Christians, weakened in faith,
were opting to revert to the old ways of Hebrew Law. In the
same way, worldly gravitational pull is constantly dragging
me back from my upward faith climb. If I take my eyes off
the prize in Jesus, relaxing my program of Christian action,
I again begin falling away.

I have tasted the goodness of the Word of God and
shared in the Holy Spirit. When I fall away, as I do daily,
will I be brought back to repentance? Verse four declares

repentance "is impossible for those who have once been enlightened." Is the writer talking about degrees here? How do we reconcile "impossible" with Jesus' words in Mark 14:36 when he cried out in His sorrowful Gethsemane prayer, *"Abba, Father, everything is possible for you"*? I have tasted that the Lord is good! I continue to witness heavenly gifts in small miracles formerly referred to as coincidences. Perhaps falling away that results from committing a violent act like murder makes it improbable for one to turn back. In my heart, though, I'm assured our Lord loves us and there is nothing we can do to change that.

For me, the final sentence of our scripture is perhaps the most difficult to assimilate. In my sobriety, I practice a spiritual program congruent with my faith in Christ. Taking a drink would create a barrier in my relationship with the One who lives in me. It would be the first shovelful of a ditch that would become a canyon separating me from my God. I would be giving up on our relationship, turning my back and walking away. The action would get me closer to snuffing out the divine pilot light within. I would be crucifying the Son of God all over again.

Abba, may we always be assured that nothing can separate us from the love of God that is in Christ Jesus. Amen.

Breakfast Fruit

Then he said to me, "Son of man, eat this scroll I am giving
you and fill your stomach with it." So I ate it, and it tasted
as sweet as honey in my mouth.
– Ezekiel 3:3

OFTEN THE TRUTH IS BITTERSWEET, AND IT
is especially hard to swallow when I'm faced with the
reality of my character defects. Even though it usually hurts
at first, my confrontation with it always leads to a sweet
awakening, for the Holy Spirit is always present in the midst
of the refiner's fire, separating *me* from the impurities of my
human condition. In the final analysis, they have already
been washed away by the blood of the Lamb. Throughout
most of life, I have been driven by dogged self-will. My stubborn insistence on doing it my "right" way was the false
idol drawing my attention away from where it should have
been: *God*.

The prophet Ezekiel, whose name means "God
Strengthens" (Maxwell Leadership Bible, 2007), was a
lighthouse beacon to the people of Israel during a most
turbulent time: their exile in Babylon. Just a few verses earlier, Yahweh refers to Israel as *obstinate and stubborn* (2:4).
Because God's chosen people had again turned away with
hardened hearts to attend to their false idols, they were
sailing onto the rocky shoals of yet another shipwreck *of
lamentation, mourning and woe* (2:10). Though the scroll

be filled with the lament of hard times and mourning, its truth will bring us back to God and our rightful place in His presence. Ezekiel's priestly habits assured his cognition of this truth. God's words were sweet as honey to his mouth.

When I have ventured away from my Creator and begun to rely on my own will with disregard for His, the truth tastes like biting into a lemon and I wince. When I begin turning my attention back to Abba, the truth is like biting into a grapefruit and it requires an additional touch of sugar. When I shed even more false idols — turning priority to scripture study, prayer and seeking the Holy Spirit through worship in fellowship — the truth becomes like a plump, succulent orange, easier to swallow. I want more of it every day.

Yahweh, may we always be turning toward You so that we might feed the sweetness of Your truth to the turbulent world around us. Amen.

DIVINE DESIRE

You have stolen my heart, my sister, my bride;
you have stolen my heart
with one glance of your eyes,
with one jewel of your necklace.
How delightful is your love, my sister, my bride!
How much more pleasing is your love than wine,
and the fragrance of your perfume
more than any spice!
Your lips drop sweetness as the honeycomb, my bride;
milk and honey are under your tongue.
The fragrance of your garments
is like the fragrance of Lebanon.
You are a garden locked up, my sister, my bride;
you are a spring enclosed, a sealed fountain.
Your plants are an orchard of pomegranates
with choice fruits,
with henna and nard,
nard and saffron,
calamus and cinnamon,
with every kind of incense tree,
with myrrh and aloes
and all the finest spices.
You are a garden fountain,
a well of flowing water
streaming down from Lebanon.
Awake, north wind,

and come, south wind!
Blow on my garden,
that its fragrance may spread everywhere.
Let my beloved come into his garden
and taste its choice fruits.
– Song of Songs 4: 9-16

O UR CREATOR, THE PSALMIST WRITES, wonderfully made us and knitted us in the womb. Individual senses miraculously cross over, influence and translate for the other senses. Never do they meld together and transcend the physical plane more than in sexual love between man and woman. Song of Songs acclaims our Father's ultimate validation of our basic instinct of procreation. In *How to Read the Bible Book by Book*, the authors state that this book "is a celebration of sexual love — and marital fidelity — between a woman and a man" (Fee and Stewart, 2002). This unique book of the Old Testament is overlooked and often avoided as subject for many Bible studies. When did you last hear your pastor preach from it? Has this part of the Word of God become distasteful to the Church?

I once gave a talk at a men's retreat titled "Life of Piety". The motivating theme in a life of piety is desire. It is life in pursuit of a more intimate relationship with our Creator. I used a popular contemporary Christian song as a lead into the presentation. Jesus Culture's "Set a Fire" voices the refrain: "Set a fire down in my soul that I can't contain, I can't control. I want more of you, God. I want more of you, God" (Reagan, 2010). This combustible intimacy we desire in our relationship with God cements a bond between husband and wife.

The disco scene of the mid '70s saw two music artists gain immense popularity and success with very sensuous and provocative songs. Barry White's big hit (with the Love Unlimited Orchestra) was titled "Can't Get Enough of Your Love, Baby," and Donna Summers' "Love to Love You, Baby" all but ushered in an era of promiscuity in the 20-something population. This period of intense secular sexual affinity was soon followed by the HIV epidemic. Some of us might have found ourselves participants in that movement and, if so, can say a prayer of gratitude for coming through it unscathed. It is clear now to this writer that no loving relationship between two people is more gratifying than when God is right in the middle of it all. From a male's perspective, C.S. Lewis said it best, "A woman's heart should be so close to God that a man should have to chase Him to find her" (Goodreads, 2021).

Abba, may we be aware of Your presence in all our intimate relationships. Amen.

Festival Day–Discernment

Who in your life growing up would you describe as "salt of the earth"? Are there people in your workplace, neighborhood or Church that you view as "salt of the earth?" Make a list. Pray for them.

Identify the instances this past week when you provided sweet content to your immediate surroundings. Were there times when you carried a sour or bitter attitude into a situation?

Where and when can you consistently find *big gulps* of spiritual milk?

What is your favorite bittersweet food?

What spiritual practice do you and your spouse use to keep God at the center of your relationship?

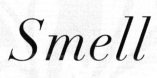

Smell

THE SCENT OF WAR

At the blast of the trumpet it snorts, "Aha!"
It catches the scent of battle from afar,
the shout of commanders and the battle cry.
— Job 39:25

I N OUR UPSIDE/DOWN WORLD, THE MOST
prosperously blessed nation on the globe is at war with itself. Recent seasons have witnessed sharp division among the populace with vitriolic derision directed at our elected President. Ours is a society where one deranged man can make a bloody battlefield out of a celebration of song. An ancient question arises again from this senseless environment: "What gives with God?"

In the story of Job, we find a similar scene enacted in one man's life. A godly man named Job, prosperous and blessed beyond measure, finds himself a victim of hard times and, in his mind, harder iniquities. Job, the definition of virtuous patience, is a biblical lesson handed down to us over generations. There permeates a recognizable aroma of self-pity in this story because Job judges his momentary afflictions unjust. Despite his troubles and with the help of Zophar, Eliphaz and Bildad (his support group), Job perseveres through relentless pursuit and petition of Yahweh.

As with Job, our default desire is to figure out life's mystery by ourselves, pulling wisdom out of our own intellect. In the end, God is wisdom's only arbiter. Today's scripture is from the first of our *Holy Bible*'s wisdom books. God, speaking to Job, sets us straight about where wisdom resides. Wisdom's first and last word remain with our Creator. God paints a picture for Job of the willing war horse's equine excitement for the impending conflict as it catches the scent of battle from afar. This animal's innate ability to take cues from its surroundings are its wisdom from God.

Oh, how easy it is for us to question our benevolent God and to doubt as the world depresses our faith. The spiritual life demands us to be more diligent in our faith walk. *"The effectual, fervent prayer of a righteous man availeth much"* (James 5:16, KJV). If we, like Job, keep seeking Yahweh, He will speak to us. Then maybe we might catch the scent of war before it is too late.

Abba, may we stay centered in the love of Your precious Son, not running headlong into conflict. Amen.

WHIFF OF JUDGEMENT

A woman in that town who lived a sinful life learned that Jesus was eating at the Pharisee's house, so she came there with an alabaster jar of perfume. As she stood behind him at his feet weeping, she began to wet his feet with her tears. Then she wiped them with her hair, kissed them and poured perfume on them.
– Luke 7:37-38

I HAVE AN OLDER MODEL HARLEY-DAVIDSON that gives me great meditative pleasure. History's great spiritual savants have all taught about the benefits of being in the present moment, remaining in the "now." Knowingly or unknowingly, this benefit is the primary attraction of motorcycle riding. In fact, if you are operating a motorcycle and you are not situated firmly in the present, you are most likely in trouble. An elevated and sharpened sense of smell is an exhilarating aspect of this pastime. For effect, I often proclaim, "When riding through the back country, I can smell grandma's apple pie cooling on the windowsill of a nearby farmhouse." Not all smells are fragrant, as some odors warn of a nearby skunk or perhaps fire danger. Our scent recognition comes by way of recollection. Our sense of smell is a door to our past. I remember a time riding when I could not identify a pleasing fragrance best described as spicy floral. Then one day, while thundering through a national forest, I recalled a childhood memory of searching the woods for roots and making sassafras tea. Soon the epiphany arrived: "Aha, sassafras, that's it!"

Searching today's scripture, I see the sinful woman (likely a prostitute), seeking validation and release from shame. She walks into a hive of Pharisees, a place where pious judgement reigns. There, reclining in the perfect peace of *now,* is the Nazarene she has heard so much about. To make her pilgrimage even more daunting, he is breathtakingly handsome! As she looked around assessing the room, she could smell the pungent odor of self-righteous indignation from the men looking down their noses at her. She proceeded anyway, white-knuckled, with her jar of perfume, for in her heart she knew there is no judgement in God's eyes. In that present moment, the now sinless woman could see in those same eyes the invitation, "Come to me and I will give you rest." Feeling unworthy as sweet grace poured over her, she cried, and her tears flowed over her Lord Jesus' feet.

Lord Jesus, thank You for seeing us as we are now, children of Your Father. May we always remember, in the midst of our shame and guilt, to look for Your reclining invitation, "Come to Me...." Amen.

SWEET SOUL SISTER

You have stolen my heart, my sister, my bride;
you have stolen my heart
with one glance of your eyes,
with one jewel of your necklace.
How delightful is your love, my sister, my bride!
How much more pleasing is your love than wine,
and the fragrance of your perfume
more than any spice!
− Song of Songs 4:9-10

IN MY CHILDHOOD HOME, WE WERE THREE brothers. Our bathroom was a boy's locker room, without the elevating fragrance of feminine hygiene. Jeanne, our mother, was the only lady of the house. Over the years, I have at times wondered what I missed by not having a sister. What would it have been like to have to share a bathroom where the only grooming item shared would be a tube of Clearasil? I have a niece, Tracy, the oldest child of my oldest brother Marty. There is not a huge gap in our ages and we have been close over the years. She often remarks that I'm the older brother she never had. She is as close as it gets for me.

Song of Songs is a book of our *Holy Bible* that appears to get passed over in most Bible studies. It touches on that visceral connection between male and female. Perhaps it is our modern culture which has distorted this instinctual attraction to engender a thread of guilt and shame into our natural desire for sexual intimacy. This beautifully sensual, poetic work, Song of Songs, is part of the Word of God that serves to guide us back again and again to a celebration of the nature of pure love between a man and a woman. With a marital fidelity component, it *is* a gift of God. *"That is why a man leaves his father and mother and is united to his wife and they become one flesh" (Genesis 2:24, NIV).*

Recently, in the fellowship of our North Georgia Walk to Emmaus, I have developed deep and loving relationships with Christian sisters. However there is one, a beautiful strawberry blonde lady, who stole my heart with one glance of her eyes. There is no doubt in either of our minds that God placed markers on each of our paths that directed us to a singular Holy encounter. He connected us through the grace of our Savior's Love. She is my sister — my bride — and we walk always surrounded by the aroma of God's eternal love for His children; sisters *and* brothers.

Abba, may all love between a man and a woman reach perfection, never again encountering the fear of the world. Amen.

FOREVER FRAGRANT

On coming to the house, they saw the child with his mother
Mary, and they bowed down and worshiped him. Then they
opened their treasures and presented him with gifts of gold,
frankincense and myrrh.
— Matthew 2:11

THE TRADITIONAL CHRISTMAS NATIVITY scene includes character figures as three wise men or kings. A classic song list for carolers regularly includes "We Three Kings". The words *gold, frankincense* and *myrrh* continually echo in my memory during each advent season. After a friend's recommendation, I recently read "The Immortal Nicholas" by Glenn Beck (2015). This nativity-centered action fantasy fostered a new curiosity in me about frankincense. Soon, I found myself buying a vanilla and frankincense candle for the same friend who recommended the book. I learned this fragrant substance, made from a resin extracted from the Boswellia tree, remains popular today. For 5,000 years, nomadic shepherds and semi-nomadic pastoralists have been collecting this aromatic resin used in perfume and incense.

Frankincense is mentioned three times in the NIV translation of the *Holy Bible*. Today's verse from the Gospel of Mathew lies between the initial reference in Exodus (30:34) and a final mention in Revelation (18:13), a historical span of over a thousand years. Now, 2,000 years hence, we light candles with a lingering redolence of a similar spirit. An ancient tree's essence of life — once considered King's treasure, an aroma pleasing to God — still enhances our life experience today.

What would the three wise men find today were they to set out in search of a traditional nativity scene? Where might they find the humble and reverent peace where a "child is born"? In the USA, they might learn it is increasingly difficult (if not impossible) to find a tried and true, live-under-the-stars nativity scene of the Child with His mother. There is no more room at the inn, and the world is pushing them aside. Let us find hope that, just as frankincense burns an aroma pleasing to God and the Bright Morning Star shines above the eastern horizon, forever the Light of Life lingers on with and in us.

Abba, may a longing for the coming again of Your precious Son burn forever in our hearts so we might bring the aroma of Christ into the world. Amen

FIVE FINGER FRIENDS

Perfume and incense bring joy to the heart, and the
pleasantness of a friend springs from their heartfelt advice.
— Proverbs 27:9

O UR HOME IN MIAMI, FLORIDA DURING THE
salad days of my youth was located on a street named
Melaleuca Lane. Our neighborhood was populated by trees
of the same name with a paper-thin, peel-away, leathery
bark. There was one of these trees standing at the end of our
driveway and it would keep me company and hide my forbidden white socks that I would quickly change into while
waiting for the morning school bus. That silent, majestic
tree was a mischievous boy's friend many a day growing up.
On the opposite side of our home, solitarily sitting in the
back yard, was the prized gardenia bush belonging to Mom
(she of the forbidden white socks' edict). In the same way
as the big melaleuca, the fragrant gardenia was a middle age
mom's quiet florally fragrant confidant.

My mother, Jeanne, was the first to teach me that over
the course of a lifetime a person could count his real friends
on one hand. This counsel rings true for me. When I reflect
on my life and identify the ones who truly trusted in me and
were always there for me...Well, I can count them with the
fingers on one hand. They are men who have been in my life
from near and afar for decades. I can go for years without
seeing or talking with each, and yet when we reconnect

it's as if no time has passed at all. Like a soothing, fragrant lotion my assurance of these folk's presence in my life, as the Message translation says, "refreshes the soul."

Many times, the wisest counsel we receive from a true friend contains no discourse, but consists only in their listening presence. A friend is someone who will always be there for us, if only to listen to our cry for help. We learn a bit about love and friendship in the Gospel of John 15:13: *"Greater love has no one than this: to lay down one's life for one's friends."* It is here in these words where we learn there is truly only one friend we require, Jesus the Christ. A wonderfully fragrant Rose of Sharon, having already laid down His life for all, waits to reign in our hearts as a silent and wonderful Counselor.

Dear Lord, open our hearts so we might invite Your Son as our silent witness to live within as the only friend we will ever need. Amen.

PEACE PIPE

*When He opened the seventh seal, there was silence in
heaven for about half an hour. And I saw the seven angels
who stand before God, and to them were given seven
trumpets. Then another angel, having a golden censer, came
and stood at the altar. He was given much incense, that he
should offer it with the prayers of all the saints upon the
golden altar which was before the throne. And the smoke of
the incense, with the prayers of the saints,
ascended before God from the angel's hand.*
– Revelation 8:1-4 (NKJV)

I GREW UP IN THE TRINITY EPISCOPAL
Church in Miami, Florida, a Byzantine-like structure
built in 1925 and nestled on Biscayne Bay. Though not
considered "high", our Church would dress up on Easter
with the Bishop leading the processional, a thurible (censer)
spewing smoke of incense swinging back and forth as they
strode down a long aisle in our cavernous sanctuary. It was
quite the pious ritual. I cannot remember the aromas, but
the sights and sounds were an extravagant banquet for the
developing senses of a young boy.

Perhaps no other book of the *Holy Bible* begs for us
to step beyond or expand our conceptual boundaries than
Revelation. It feeds all our senses with images that have min-
imal earthly equivalents. I am reminded of the first time my
medicine man friend Tom invited me to a Native American

pipe ceremony. A pipe with traditional tobacco was passed around a "sacred circle" of men while seated in the woods close to nature. Tom modeled what we were to do when the pipe was handed to us. I watched as he, in the Lakota tribe fashion, entreated *Wakan Tanka* with his prayers. My first time at one of these ceremonies, I struggled to expand my conceptual boundaries. I can imagine it is the same for any adult their first time attending a church service.

Since the beginning of mankind, smoke with its natural desire to rise upward has carried human hopes and prayers towards our sacred and divine Creator. Beginning with the book of Genesis, one will see hundreds of references to burnt offerings and, likewise, the word *incense*. I have no doubts that — just as in prayerful worship on Sundays in church — our triune God was, is and will always be present in the Native American sacred circle as they pass what might also be called the *Prince of Peace* pipe.

Wakan Tanka, thank You for sending Your angels to guide us, so our prayers ascend before You and might be gathered together with those of all the saints. Amen.

Festival Day–Discernment

Why does God allow bad things to happen to good people?

Have you ever have caught the scent of a conflict before it arrived? When?

What kind of activities help you stay situated and centered in the present moment? In what ways are your senses heightened? Can you cite an example?

Where have you noticed Christian traditions and symbols being squeezed out of contemporary culture? What symbols or traditions have weathered the centuries and remain steadfast today?

When was the last time you counted your friends? Write a note to a friend you haven't been in touch with for a long time.

Do you know someone who does not profess to be a Christian or is unchurched, so to speak, but still exhibits qualities that suggest Jesus?

See

ONE UNSEEN TRUTH

*Therefore, we do not lose heart. Though outwardly we are
wasting away, yet inwardly we are being renewed day by
day. For our light and momentary troubles are achieving for
us an eternal glory that far outweighs them all. So we fix
our eyes not on what is seen, but on what is unseen, since
what is seen is temporary, but what is unseen is eternal.*
– 2 Corinthians 4:16-18

IN THE EARLY 1970'S AS A COLLEGE STUDENT
on the cusp of a University of Georgia undergraduate
degree in Journalism, I was typically impressionable and
idealistic. We were coming out of the unpopular Vietnam
War. Psychedelics and protests were prevalent, and I was
facing transition into serious adulthood. As I look back
now, the world in those days was also upside/down. I had
recently turned legal drinking age and, in my short life, I
had lived through one American President's assassination
and was watching another being run out of office. There
was a common popular idiom making the rounds: "Believe
nothing you hear and only half of what you see."

During this time frame, a song writer that I grew up
listening to, Stevie Wonder, released an album titled
Innervisions. It was a seminal event in the evolution of my
spiritual growth and developing faith. I wore out a stylus
playing that album. The music and the message in the lyrics
never lost its shine or glow with me and still hasn't. It was

the first time it ever occurred to me, like the album title stated so revealingly, that there exists in humans an inner vision. We all have it. We just need to awaken to it. In that day, Stevie Wonder had fully awakened to his "Innervisions". With no physical sight, he penned songs that exactly captured what the world was seeing during that era. He could not fix his eyes on what was seen; instead, he saw the truth in what was unseen.

When we begin to lose heart, our eyes lowering below the horizon, our artist Creator speaks to us through His earthly artist angels: Copeland, Van Gogh, Shakespeare, Wonder. Truth, born out in watercolors, sharp notes and flowing descriptive, carries an unseen eternal reality to our senses and it resonates in our collective soul. We are moved and renewed, moving day by day closer to our God and His eternal glory.

Yahweh, we pray that we would awaken to the truth embodied in Your precious Son and it would resonate in our soul forever. Amen.

A FAVORABLE VIEW

*Now therefore, I pray, if I have found grace in Your sight,
show me now Your way, that I may know You and that
I may find grace in Your sight. And consider that
this nation is Your people.*
— Exodus 33:13 (NKJV)

D O YOU THINK MOSES WAS A FRUSTRATED man when he emerged from Mount Horeb with the divine tablets and saw his people dancing around a golden calf? Didn't these same people just witness the Red Sea's waters part, facilitating their escape from slavery? For sure, his temper flared and he flung the priceless Ten Commandments to the ground. Moses saw himself as an Israelite. The people were a part of him and he was a part of the people. Moses turned back to God once again.

Today, one of our culture's golden calves is *fame* — a desire to become celebrated, achieve notoriety, be elevated above the common and mundane. It is a ladder-climbing endeavor peppered with the spice of rich images put forth by what car we drive, where we live, our job title, the school our kids go to and sometimes the spouse we marry. We chase a self-image forged in the fire of what other people will think of us; in other words, how we appear in other's eyes.

Perhaps Moses' initial motivation for a return conversation with God was to persuade Yahweh to not find him guilty by association with the folks partying around a stupid bovine. We can dismiss this idea because clearly this next conversation is all about the personal relationship between Moses and God. Moses, ever humble and teachable, implores Yahweh, "Show me," or, "Teach me your ways." After the initial shock and irritation of witnessing the foolish behavior of his people, Moses thinks first about how *God* sees him, not how they view him. He then petitions to find favor in God's sight.

The question of Moses *finding favor in God's sight,* or in some translations, *finding grace in God's sight,* becomes moot with the birth, death and resurrection of Christ our Savior. By His life, Jesus showed that our Heavenly Father loves us no matter what. In fact, we do not have to do anything to merit His covering grace. It is our simple act of turning and accepting that which opens the gates of this magnificent gift. Then we will see we have found favor in His eyes.

Father, help us to discard our need to look good in other people's eyes and know we will always find favor when we turn again to look in Your eyes. Amen.

PLOW AHEAD

*Jesus replied, "No one who puts a hand to the plow and
looks back is fit for service in the kingdom of God."*
– Luke 9:62

D URING MY MOST FORMATIVE YEARS I WAS
a surfer boy spending hours in the Atlantic Ocean as
it readied to kiss the shore adjacent to Miami's South Beach
Pier. The only looking back I did was studying the swell patterns so I might catch the best of the approaching breakers.
Sitting on my surfboard was akin to sitting on my motorcycle. My life then was all ahead of me. There was little past
to look back on nor the need to do so. As young boys are
want to do, I savored every moment!

Motorcycling like surfing is a pastime that stimulates all
of one's senses. The touch of the wind on your face or the
rumble of the engine in your ears invigorates. It is a means
of peace and a ride through the countryside always becomes
my stress reliever. When riding wave or motorcycle, each
instant is a wonderful opportunity for prayerful worship
in the beauty of His Creation. Amid our exhilaration however, we must not let our eyes wander. One of the most valuable motorcycle riding tenets taught in training classes and
one that holds true for both sports is: "Wherever you look,
that is where your bike (board) will go." In the same way, if
we keep our eyes on the Father, our life's ride will go more
smoothly! Ancient farmers who toiled behind oxen or plow

horses understood that they had to keep their eyes planted on the immediate row ahead to guide animal and plow in the preferred line.

The retired view of life while entering the second half of my sixties comes from a much different angle than when I was entering the second half of my teens, heading into college. Jesus's words from today's scripture came in the first half of His thirties on the way to Jerusalem, where He already knew His life here would end there. His was a mission from His Father to save the world. He did not rest on the laurels of His prior miracles, nor did He divert His path or delay progress for fear of His impending crucifixion. Keeping his eyes on the prize he taught us, "Each day has enough trouble of its own" (Matthew 6:34).

Yahweh, help us remember to not look back, so we might see through the eyes of Jesus and remain in Your presence one day at a time. Amen.

Daddy Winks

*He looked up and said, "I see people; they look like trees
walking around." Once more Jesus put his hands on the
man's eyes. Then his eyes were opened, his sight was restored,
and he saw everything clearly.*
– Mark 8:24-25

Today's verses come soon after Jesus
had an exchange with His disciples. It is an exclama-
tory back-and-forth and Jesus, frustrated, asks, "Are your
hearts hardened? Do you have eyes but fail to see?" (v.17).
I empathize with Jesus and want to ask, "I mean, really? Hey
guys, remember the walking on water and the fishes and
loaves?" Then Jesus did what He has always done, what He
continues to do and what He will always do with us when
we are willing. He snaps His fingers, wakes us up and cures
our blindness.

I do not have to be completely blacked-out blind to
miss all that our Father presents to me daily. I just need
a little hardening of the heart. It might be a small irritation from someone fumbling with their payment in a
long, slowing grocery checkout line or a driver following
too closely, honking the horn. There is no way I am seeing
what Jesus wants me to see in those situations. These people
might as well be trees walking around in my rear view and
God needs to grab me by the shoulders and spit in my eye!

When the ever-loving hands of Immanuel are on me, I am brought back into the moment where my vision is restored, and I begin to see clearly once again. What I can then see are the little miracles I used to refer to as coincidences. My faith has brought me to a place where I take nothing for granted. One day I was standing in the checkout line at a local grocery store and movement was just slow enough to allow me to notice the cashier's name was Jeanne, my mother's name. I decided I wanted to shop there again. The next time I was there in line the cashier's name was Betty, same as my mom's sister, who was also my godmother. Now it is the store where I do all my grocery shopping!

Abba, we long for Your Son's touch to slow us down enough so we can see You always winking at us. Amen.

SIGHT EFFECTS

I have seen everything in my days of vanity: There is a just man who perishes in his righteousness, and there is a wicked man who prolongs life in his wickedness.
— Ecclesiastes 7:15 (NKJV)

THE 1960S WERE QUITE A TIME FOR AN American boy to be transitioning from teenager into young man. In junior high, kids used the word *conceited* when describing classmates who were enamored with themselves. This adolescent variety of vanity had coolness as its core desire. Walking in Bass Weejuns and wearing Gant shirts with Butch Wax-spiked hair was key to being seen as cool. Amid this vanity of coolness sprang an American folk-rock group called The Byrds. One of their most popular hits was "Turn, Turn, Turn." The record reached number one on the Billboard charts in December 1965. Soon afterward, I learned this song was based on a book of the Old Testament Bible. Not long after I sought and found some sense in Ecclesiastes 3:1-8, the scripture opened a boy's eyes enough to realize maybe there was something more to this Bible thing. Even back then, Abba was winking at me.

The entire book of wisdom that is Ecclesiastes is not an easy read and hard to make sense of. I am glad my first venture into it was that declaration in chapter three, verse one, *"To everything there is a season..."* If I had first stumbled upon today's devotion scripture, I might never have returned to read Ecclesiastes another day. I am now truly coming into my season of faith. In those days of little faith, all was vanity.

The word *vanity* appears in the NKJV translation of the *Holy Bible* thirty-three times, and thirty-one are found in Ecclesiastes. The pre-Christ message of Ecclesiastes speaks to me: "*You can't take it with you!*" The recurrent admonition, *"For all is vanity and grasping for the wind"* (1:14, 2:17), becomes moot with the birth of the Christ child. The upside/down observations about the righteous and the wicked are viewed through the eyes of the vain. When I am seeing through eyes of vanity I am seeing the picture frame, not the picture. The body is the frame and the soul, the picture. Until I become more concerned with how God sees me rather than how others see me, I will struggle with vanity. I will grasp at thin air. More importantly, my concern today is: How do I see myself? When Christ abides in me, I can see myself through His forgiving eyes, the eyes of eternal love.

Father, open our eyes so the only wind we grasp at is the breath of the Holy Spirit. Amen

COME AND SEE

*Philip found Nathanael and told him, "We have found the
one Moses wrote about in the Law, and about whom the
prophets also wrote—Jesus of Nazareth, the
son of Joseph."*

*"Nazareth! Can anything good come from there?"
Nathanael asked.*

"Come and see," said Philip.

*When Jesus saw Nathanael approaching, he said of him,
"Here truly is an Israelite in whom there is no deceit."*

"How do you know me?" Nathanael asked.

*Jesus answered, "I saw you while you were still under the
fig tree before Philip called you."*
–John 1:45-48

I ONCE GAVE A TALK ON CHRISTIAN ACTION
to a room full of Christian men. In its early composition
stages, I struggled with getting my creativity flowing. My
first connotation about Christian action contained images
of service, volunteering in the context of the church. I have
been an usher and have participated in annual Bar-B-Que
fundraisers. I have been a member of the church finance

committee and sat on the church council, all of which many would consider as Christian action. Most of my motivation in the infancy of my faith was based upon making sure I was seen engaged, participating and busy.

If someone were to ask me to talk about Jesus's calling of the disciples, I would most certainly speak first of, well, the first called: Simon (Peter) and his brother Andrew! In fact, if asked to name the twelve disciples, I would be hard pressed to even remember Nathanael. What was Nathanael doing when Jesus first noticed him? Nothing, just chilling under a fig tree. Not only was he doing nothing, but when Philip grabbed his attention his first reaction was a purely skeptical bias toward folk from Nazareth. How dare anyone bother him while he is isolating!

My beginning idea of Christian action conjured up images of proselytizing sidewalk preachers in scripture-laden sandwich boards proclaiming, "Repent, for the time is near!" However, I had been given a talk outline to follow which included the foundational scripture, *"I am the way, the truth and the life"* from John 14:6. From these words of Jesus, I sculpted a talk around the concept that how we comport ourselves is always our most important action. In fact, it is the people we are least likely to be aware of that notice us. Nathanael just happened to be noticed by the One Moses wrote about in the law. What was Nathanael doing under that fig tree? When does Christ notice us the most? For this writer, it is when I am living in the Way and the Way is living in me. Or perhaps it is better said: when I am noticing Him.

Messiah, may we find our fig tree, so we might be still and know that You are God. Amen.

Festival Day – Discernment

How has music and art played a role in your spiritual journey? How does the Holy Spirit speak to you through the creative arts?

How do spiritual disciplines like fasting help us to be more concerned about how God sees us, rather than how other people view us?

What are some activities can we engage in that demand we stay in the present moment?

How does our vanity show up on a daily basis to keep us from seeing what God is providing for us in each and every moment?

When was the last time someone you did not even know noticed you for the way you are?

Hear

GOD'S EVOLVING CALL

Then the word of the Lord came to Jonah a second time:
"Go to the great city of Nineveh and proclaim to it the
message I give you."

Jonah obeyed the word of the Lord and went to Nineveh.
Now Nineveh was a very large city; it took three days to go
through it. Jonah began by going a day's journey into the
city, proclaiming, "Forty more days and Nineveh will be
overthrown." The Ninevites believed God.
A fast was proclaimed, and all of them, from the greatest
to the least, put on sackcloth.
– Jonah 3:1-5

EVEN IN MY MOST SERIOUS MOMENTS OF Bible study, when I come across Jonah I cannot help but relive those childhood images from the big screen of Pinocchio in the belly of the whale. My guess is that for many, these cinematic portrayals are the closest they will get to the treasure trove of truth that is the Bible. This could easily have been my case, as well. I am grateful my parents pointed me to the Church as a child, as well as to the lessons Pinocchio laid before me.

From my most recent reading of Jonah in preparation for this devotion, I noticed something new. The scripture speaks to me this way: When the word of the Lord comes to Jonah the second time –after the fish experience — it

has changed from when it came to him the first tin
hears something quite different the second time. I
"preach against" (NIV) or *"cry out against"* (NKJ\ ) from
the first call found in verse 2 of chapter 1, Jonah hears:
"Proclaim to" and, *"Preach to"* Nineveh.

Is it God's call changing, or is it Jonah changing? I
believe we hear God's call differently as we grow in our faith
and spirituality. Does God's call differ from His will? Just
as His abundant, loving grace is eternal and constant, so is
His will for us. The trials and tribulations of our lives can
cause us to grow and turn back toward our Creator. The
second time, Jonah obeyed and went to Nineveh. Whether
through the belly the whale or refiner's fire, we grow in
faith and maybe we hear His call the second time, or maybe
we hear it the third time. I heard God's call from Pinocchio
as a child and understood how important it was not to lie,
and then I heard it differently when I read the book of
Jonah for the first time.

*Father may our eyes always be open to see and our ears to hear
Your constant and eternal message to us. Amen.*

FAMILY KEEPSAKES

For there is nothing hidden that will not be disclosed,
and nothing concealed that will not be known or
brought out into the open.
— Luke 8:17

I DON'T KNOW WHAT THE BOOK IS ON MOTH-er-son conversations, especially the mother-teenager son type. My guess is that there is a much deeper reservoir of information when it comes to father-son or mother-daughter exchanges. But here we were, my mom Jeanne and I, in a quiet, God-filled moment when a family secret was revealed. Maybe the revelation could have been a father-son type, but my dad had died a couple of years earlier. For sure, I know there was some redemption for this woman pouring out her soul to her youngest child.

She prefaced her monologue with a lesson on the value and importance of telling the truth. One never gets used to seeing his mother cry, and it was the first time I remembered her crying in this way. She told of being raised by her grandmother, except that Jeanne thought her grandmother was her mother and her mother was her sister.

I think it might have been the first time I ever heard the term "illegitimate child". Good God Almighty, how in the world did we, as a cultured society, ever come up with that false premise!? The worst part, as today's scripture verse says, is that "*nothing is secret that will not be revealed.*" My mother went on to say that the secret was revealed when she was around the age of ten. From the chiding voices of playmates on the school ground play yard, she heard for the first time the shattering truth that her sister was really her mom.

The fact that the truth hurts is an actual reality of our lives. Here is what occurs when we try to hide it: a much greater pain and chaos and more people affected! A dark cycle begins that runs through successive generations. Children born out of wedlock were a reality in my mother's family for Jeanne, then a son and a granddaughter. The original lie, given time to grow, has twice repeated the cycle. The only truth lives in the belief that God has no illegitimate children, for we are all children of God! His only begotten Son has told us so.

Father, guide us away from our desires to deny what is true. Help us to look first inside ourselves to know that, at our core, You are our creator and there can never be anything illegitimate about this truth. Amen.

SEASONED GRACE

*Likewise, the tongue is a small part of the body, but it
makes great boasts. Consider what a great forest is set
on fire by a small spark.*
– James 3:5

*Let your conversation be always full of grace, seasoned with
salt, so that you may know how to answer everyone.*
– Colossians 4:6

IN OCTOBER 1987 I WAS SENT BY MY EMPLOYER,
Marriott Corporation, to what was known as the
Management ID training program. ID was an acronym
for Individual Development. The experience was memo-
rable on many levels. It was my first trip to our nation's cap-
ital, Marriott Headquarters being in Bethesda, Maryland,
a northwestern suburb of D.C. Our first full day of class-
work was Monday, October 19th, also known as "Black
Monday," the greatest single day percentage market drop
on Wall Street in history. I was amazed when Bill Marriott,
Jr., Marriott Chairman of the Board, took time to pay a visit
to the company's newest crop of managers. I sat stunned as
this remarkable man of faith, certainly aware that millions
of dollars of his wealth were evaporating, calmly and confi-
dently welcomed us to the company. His words to my ears
were full of grace, seasoned with salt.

During the training one day, we all formed a circle and practiced an exercise that would illustrate how a message can become warped over a short period of time as it passes from one to another. The first person is given a statement and then whispers it into the ear of the next person and it is passed to the next in the same way until it finally gets to the final messenger, when it practically has no relation to its original meaning or context. Were the beginning message a petty rumor, one could see how, by the time it made its rounds, it might be the small spark news igniting the great figurative forest fire. Similarly, our stock markets are kindling combustible to the kneejerk spark of rumor and panic that results in a plaintive cry of "SELL!"

My years in broadcasting taught me a skill in the art of inflection as a communication tool. I have learned painfully over time that this skill can get me in trouble. It all starts with me not being at peace in the present moment which leads to poor listening, a volatile catalyst for massive miscommunication. Emotion falls as pepper on the conversation and I have no answer for putting out the subsequent, unnecessary fire.

Father, may we hold our tongues long enough to receive truth and answer in a graceful salt of the earth way. Amen.

TOTALLY CONNECTED

Come to me, all you who are weary and burdened,
and I will give you rest.
– Matthew 11:28

I ONCE BOUGHT INTO THE PREMISE, "IT'S NOT what you know. It's who you know." I heard those words from my mother more than once. When one seeks to climb the corporate ladder, having the right connections is valuable. The statement is particularly true in the political arena and the basis of how the world defines success. I got lost chasing this illusion because I did not realize the "who" I needed to know was God!

We were meant to be in fellowship, joined together in common purpose, linked to one another, connected to something greater and more meaningful than our unsettled selves. We have all longed to find our somewhere, a place where we belong. We long to become whole, complete, one. This quest becomes so self-centered that it sometimes boils down to a simple effort to be comfortable in our own skin, the rest that Jesus offers us.

In the summer of 2017, North America experienced a rare total eclipse of the sun. The path of totality crossed the entire continent from west to east, which had not occurred since 1918. Researching the mystery of this celestial wonder, I learned a new amazingly spiritual, yet scientific word. *Syzygy* is a celestial phenomenon where three bodies — sun, moon and earth — reach perfect alignment (Merriam-Webster, 2021).

On Monday, August 21, I found myself in Andrews, N.C., amidst a festival day atmosphere with many a pilgrim, young and old, gazing upward in awestruck wonder. Andrews was point zero in the exact center of the path of totality. I discovered *syzygy* is not complete; not whole nor total. It does not reach its fullness without humanity — us, as receiving witnesses — the fourth body in alignment. God called us to align with His will. Right at the point of total eclipse it became quiet, still, totally silent, and very peaceful. There, on the exterior of the Andrews UMC, was a large sign with the words of today's scripture. I caught a glimpse of the rest Jesus was referring to that day and I heard from God further in verses 29-30, for the Greek origin of the word *syzygy* means *yoke together* (Merriam-Webster, 2021).

Yahweh, may we stay close enough to Your Son to be in the shadow of Your eternal presence. Amen.

SEEKING IS BELIEVING

In my distress I called to the Lord;
I cried to my God for help.
From his temple he heard my voice;
my cry came before him, into his ears.
– Psalm 18:6

IN THE LATE SEVENTIES I WAS PUBLIC
Relations Director for a NASCAR Winston Cup Grand
National racing team. I had experience in sports television,
but my knowledge and familiarity with stock car racing was
limited and green as our number 88 race car. I remember
pulling up to our shop one morning, where I was greeted by
an ear-splitting roar coming from the back of the building.
Our engine builder, an unassuming South Carolinian
known as "Ducky" Newman, was testing a newly assem-
bled race engine on the team's dynamometer. The high tech
measuring device would provide all sorts of graphs and read
outs, but it was the cry of his engine creations that would
speak as music to Ducky's ears.

It is difficult for me to imagine how — in this immea-
surable universe, on this vast planet I call home, along with
over seven billion other souls — our Creator would hear my
voice. My faith does not require me to see or even imagine
something to be able to believe it. It does require that I continue to seek God. For if I continue to seek my Father, He
will reveal Himself to me in small miracles. The more I am

awakened to the Holy Spirit within, the more I will have noticed miracles I used to refer to as small world coincidences. Then, in my time of distress, I become assured God hears my voice.

One day, I was at Daytona International Speedway in the pits with our race team. I was standing next to Ducky. Our car, with his engine in it, was in practice on the track with twenty or so other very loud machines. I watched in amazement as Ducky, sitting on the pit wall with his back to the track, would tell me each time our car would pass by, making another lap. All the race cars sounded alike to me. Ducky knew his creation. His engine had a sound unique to itself and Ducky could hear it as if a voice were calling to him. And so it is with us when, in our search, we call to the Lord.

Father God, we pray that we would always be in seeking mode, so our voice will be music to Your ears. Amen.

CODE WORDS

What you heard from me, keep as the pattern of sound
teaching, with faith and love in Christ Jesus. Guard the
good deposit that was entrusted to you—guard it with the
help of the Holy Spirit who lives in us.
— 2 Timothy 1:13-14

I N THE FALL OF 1970, AS A FRESHMAN AT THE
University of Georgia, I joined a Greek system on
campus fraternity. My older brother Hal and some other
high school friends already belonged, but I was not assured
a bid to join. After my invitation to join, there was an
intense ritualistic initiation process complete with slight
hazing. Our class, still boys, rote-learned a loyalty pledge
that included the code words "a brother in the bond." It was
not of sound teaching! This is where I regretfully experienced a way of the world and learned the meaning of "black
balled." Membership in our separate and somewhat secret
society had a voting process where exclusion would occur
with a bad faith deposit of a black marble into a passed
ballot box.

In the second letter to his protégée Timothy, Paul
beseeches him to avoid joining in the way of the world.
Their still young brotherhood, rooted in faith and love, had
a not-so-secret charge of saving humanity. Paul was trying
to pass on to the next generation, Timothy's generation, a
concept entirely new and never before tried. The concept

was inclusion. With the advent of Christ and the Gospel Way concerning humanity, the need for the word *include* becomes obsolete! Love excludes no one. A synonym of inclusion is *encompassing* (Merriam-Webster, 2021). Love is all encompassing. There is no need for black balls!

If I am to hold fast to the sound teachings of Jesus the Christ, I must first be loyal and devoted to the truth, ever seeking it in all situations. Second, I need help. I cannot do it alone. I find help in various fellowships. These fellowships will never survive on an exclusionary basis, because the truth which arrives on the wings of the Holy Spirit can never fully present itself in an unaccepting environment. He taught us this very truth in Matthew 18:20.

Father, may we always guard Your good deposit and know the only code words we will ever need are "I love You!" Amen.

Festival Day – Discernment

Can you recall a time when you have heard or read a familiar Bible verse and it spoke to you in a new way?

Do you have any secrets that need to be revealed? Plan to share them soon with someone you trust.

Have you recently heard yourself speak, only to realize afterward that the words should have been seasoned with a little grace? When was the last time you wish you had held your tongue?

Are you at peace, comfortable in your own skin? If not, how long has it been since you felt that way? What will it take to get back to that place?

Are you a member of any groups that set themselves above others and are perhaps exclusionary? How can your presence make them more Christ-like and inclusive?

Touch

TWO IN TOUCH

*This is the word that came to Jeremiah from the Lord: "Go
down to the potter's house, and there I will give you my
message." So I went down to the potter's house, and I saw
him working at the wheel. But the pot he was shaping from
the clay was marred in his hands; so the potter formed it
into another pot, shaping it as seemed best to him.*

*Then the word of the Lord came to me. He said,
"Can I not do with you, Israel, as this potter does?"
declares the Lord. "Like clay in the hand of the potter,
so are you in my hand, Israel.*
– Jeremiah 18:1-6

I HAD JUST BECOME A TEENAGER AND WAS
fast discovering girls when one of the great love songs of
all time, "Unchained Melody", was the hit of the summer. It
made the Righteous Brothers a household name. The lyrics
include the line: "I've hungered for your touch." It was one
of the most internationally recorded songs of all time; a
steadfast jukebox standard. A quarter century later —
almost forgotten — it showed up in the soundtrack of
the blockbuster movie *Ghost* as background to a famously
steamy potter's wheel scene. This wonderful musical
creation was reborn.

Our hunger for the Potter's touch is no less urgent when
we come to the place where we have forgotten who we are

and from whence we came. Then *we* are trying to control the shaping and molding of our lives, the caution lights flash and red flags begin to fly. My most common red flag is the desire to isolate. I am inclined to stay inside the house and inside myself. I don't want to see nor talk to anyone. There are immediate remedies for me, at my fingertips. The question is whether I will act and employ the tools and methods available to me or whether I will let fear of surrender and submission paralyze, letting laziness set in. The solution is as simple as picking up the phone.

Our Father made us to be in fellowship, and it only takes two (see Matthew 18:20). In the famous scene from *Ghost,* a man and woman deeply in love with each other find a most intimate connection with the Holy Spirit. But it is in the everyday interaction with family, friends and the community of faith where we find the divine connection of the Holy Spirit — the Potter's touch — preparing our marred clay to be made again into another vessel.

Yahweh, may we remember that Your touch is most healing when two or more are together as one. Amen.

TURNING POINT

So Jacob was left alone, and a man wrestled with him till daybreak. When the man saw that he could not overpower him, he touched the socket of Jacob's hip so that his hip was wrenched as he wrestled with the man. Then the man said, "Let me go, for it is daybreak." But Jacob replied, "I will not let you go unless you bless me. The man asked him, "What is your name?" "Jacob," he answered.

Then the man said, "Your name will no longer be Jacob, but Israel, because you have struggled with God and with humans and have overcome."

Jacob said, "Please tell me your name." But he replied, "Why do you ask my name?" Then he blessed him there. So Jacob called the place Peniel, saying, "It is because I saw God face to face, and yet my life was spared."
– Genesis 32:24-30

A LAYMAN'S VIEW OF COLLEGIATE WRES-
tling would likely not include the descriptor *nuanced*. Yet, the sport of wrestling is indeed infused with nuance. Revered Swiss psychiatrist Carl Jung once stated in so many words, "What you resist, persists." So it is our nuanced surrender in a wrestling match that will often lead to a victory over an opponent.

In our famously familiar scripture of Jacob wrestling with God, we find a major Old Testament turning point. There are many emotions Jacob feels as he approaches a meeting with his brother Esau, but his fear (v.7) is most prevalent. This fear often touches us in paralyzing ways, causing us to become inert. What did Jacob do? He sought stillness in solitude and turned his faith into prayer. From the promised seed and one representing the chosen lineage, he undergoes a change in character. He prevails in his struggles and God proclaims, *"Your name shall no longer be called Jacob, but Israel"* (v. 28). The payoff: two brothers' graceful, embracing reconciliation.

Our wrestling coach in high school, Major Worsham, was a WWII veteran and biology professor who preached Darwin's survival of the fittest. He was a stern taskmaster who knew how and when to show a group of boys (who would be men) the love of Christ. There would come a critical time in each and every match where we would need to have that *nuanced touch*, a split-second disciplined decision, a scant moment of surrender, the pause of resistance where we would use our opponent's own strength against them. It would be the turning point, the difference in victory. In the same way, Luke Worsham knew exactly when to show us love, and it touched us deep in our then-maturing psyches. In fact, he loved our 1970 team into a conference and national championship.

Father, may we learn from Jacob and recognize when it is time for us to surrender and let Thy will, not ours be done. Amen.

THE WORTHY CARPENTER

When the people saw that Moses was so long in coming down from the mountain, they gathered around Aaron and said, "Come, make us gods who will go before us. As for this fellow Moses who brought us up out of Egypt, we don't know what has happened to him."

Aaron answered them, "Take off the gold earrings that your wives, your sons and your daughters are wearing, and bring them to me." So all the people took off their earrings and brought them to Aaron. He took what they handed him and made it into an idol cast in the shape of a calf, fashioning it with a tool. Then they said, "These are your gods, Israel, who brought you up out of Egypt."
– Exodus 32:1-4

I HAVE A FRIEND NAMED TOM WHO HAS HIS own home remodeling business. His profession is not one that required years of college, nor a fancy diploma. It is work that requires a skillful touch in crafting cabinets, as well as building personal relationships. He has been successful because of what he does with his hands and how he keeps his word. He is a student of Native American spiritualism and you will find art around his home that reflects the culture of these original inhabitants of North America. I refer to Tom as the "Medicine Man". Although he does not profess to follow Jesus, I can see the spirit of Jesus in him.

He possesses and maintains the fruits of the spirit, especially patience.

Our scripture passage from Exodus gives us a lesson in patience. Here we have the Israelites — God's chosen people, fresh from deliverance out of Egyptian slavery through the miraculous, parting waters of the Red Sea — and they cannot even wait a couple of days for the deliverer to return from having a conversation with the same God who delivered them. Can you say, "Duh, Israelites"?

Today, we are no different than these forgetful people. Examples in my life are too many to count. On the heels of some good fortune, I've contentedly lost sight of the source of my blessings and become distracted by worldly voices, as a sailor wooed by the seductive song of sea sirens. What compounds this puzzling dilemma even more is that those Israelites, unlike us, could not draw from the added foundational benefit of the wisdom of the risen Christ.

So how is it going to be for you and me? Whether we are on the mountain top with Moses or in the valley with Aaron, we will always be given the same choices. We can either take the easiest expedient distraction, or we can wait for the Word. In our patient seeking for the answers, we might even notice a humble carpenter walking along the seashore. Now we can choose to embrace the Worthy Lamb, not the golden calf.

Father, we pray the hands of Your craftsman Son will continually mold and shape us into the model that represents You in this world. Amen.

HOLDING HANDS

For I am the LORD your God
who takes hold of your right hand
and says to you, Do not fear;
I will help you.
– Isaiah 41:13

HAVE YOU EVER SAT IN CHURCH NEXT TO someone you love deeply, certain the two of you share the same reason for being there? You both share a desire for more in a relationship with Yahweh. Reaching for your loved one's hand begins a joint beckoning of the Holy Spirit to kindle the fire of His love within. Maybe I was not awakened, for I do not remember an experience such as this until I was in my sixties. Sometimes, as prayer begins she reaches for my hand. Other times I provide the impetus. Never does a worship service end wherein our hands have not held each other's.

The poetic words of the prophet Isaiah throughout his book soothe us with a simplistic approach to understanding God's majestic love for us. The only action we need to take is to reach out our hand. Nothing else in the universe is as mutually, two-way comforting as an offered touch accepted. Surely nothing can please our Creator more than one of His children accepting the eternal overture of His wondrous grace. We will know there is nothing to fear.

Consider for a moment this same proposition welcomed by two or more gathered who are reaching together in prayerful acceptance. If I arrive early enough for the contemporary worship service at Smyrna First UMC, I will witness our praise band in a hand-held prayer circle shortly before they take the stage. I can feel the grace emanating from that space. In no time, the Holy Spirit is abiding in me and again I begin to know the love God has for me. The fourth chapter of 1 John is a rich love lesson, and in it we will find this promise: *"God is love, and he who abides in love abides in God, and God in him"* (v.16, NKJV). The power found in this promise is exponential when we change it to read, "And they who abide in love..." Hold my hand.

Yahweh grant that we would always know with certainty that when we hold Your hand, all things are possible. Amen.

LOVE SIGNS

That which was from the beginning, which we have heard,
which we have seen with our eyes, which we have looked
at and our hands have touched—this we proclaim
concerning the Word of life.
– 1 John 1:1

THE ORIGINAL SEEDS OF CHRISTIANITY were still being sown when the verse for today's devotion was written. The writer was talking about Jesus, right? But when he says *we,* is he talking about the original twelve disciples or current apostles leading the movement? What about the statement, *"...and our hands have touched"*? It is easy to believe that yes, the disciples touched Jesus, for they were constantly with him. Apostles who came to the movement later, like Paul, never touched Jesus. So what does John, who also writes, *"which we have seen with our own eyes,"* mean? Or Is he just using figurative language?

At the age of sixty-five, I participated in my very first Christian mission trip outside of the United States. I found myself in Haiti with a team of eight other people. Seven of these people had served this same medical mission for many years. We traveled with a group of Haitian men who provided support, which included being our interpreters with the patients. One day we went to a place where no one, including the Haitian men, had ever been. It was called Haiti Deaf Academy. Our patients this day were the child residents of this amazing school. It did not take long for our interpreters to realize that their practiced skills were rendered pointless. There would be no spoken words needing translation. Initially, there was a little confusion; then Christ arrived. The joyful students became the teachers, gravitating to their countrymen brothers. Hands and fingers became a dance of words, music to the eyes of the heart. In the speechless silence, the hand of God reached in and touched our souls. We learned, without a doubt, that the Word of Life manifested in the language of love needs no translation!

My primary responsibility on the team was in our optical clinic, assembling eyeglasses with the proper corrective lenses. This day at the Deaf School was the only time in over a week when I had no glasses to craft. As I reflected on this awesome day of grace it occurred to me, *Our God knew these beautiful children were without hearing and speech, so He made sure to give them excellent eyesight!* Hallelujah.

Abba, we pray daily to find the quiet place where we can hear and be touched by the language of Your Son's Love. Amen.

OUR SALVIFIC TEARS

Then one of the elders asked me, "These in white robes—
who are they, and where did they come from?" I answered,
"Sir, you know."

And he said, "These are they who have come out of the
great tribulation; they have washed their robes and made
them white in the blood of the Lamb. Therefore,

"they are before the throne of God
and serve him day and night in his temple;
and he who sits on the throne
will shelter them with his presence.
'Never again will they hunger;
never again will they thirst.
The sun will not beat down on them,'
nor any scorching heat.
For the Lamb at the center of the throne
will be their shepherd;
'he will lead them to springs of living water.'
'And God will wipe away every tear from their eyes.'"
– Revelation 7:13-17

HAVE YOU EVER SEEN A GROWN MAN CRY?
Why is it not fashionable for crying to accompany
masculinity? What is so toxic about a man crying? Why
are tears salty and not sweet? Why do I make such effort to

hide or disguise them when, in fact, they have such a salvific effect for me? These ponderings confound me almost as much as the Revelation images of trumpets, white robes, elders and thrones! Certainly, there are not many actions more graceful than the gesture offering of tissues when another has tears rolling down both cheeks. Witnessing this transaction occur between two men is downright otherworldly, and you might want to have a tissue available to wipe away your own tears!

While preparing for my first international mission trip I learned that our destination, Haiti, had the second highest infant/maternal mortality rate in the world, second only to war-ravaged Afghanistan. I wanted to cry. Upon arriving there, all my senses were subject to varying degrees of recalibration. Everything had to be reinterpreted. I did not know the language, had little taste for the food, the smells were mostly indescribable, and I could not rationally explain most of what I was seeing. Even though a decade had passed since the 2010 catastrophic 7.0 earthquake, it looked as though it happened just months before. Everywhere I turned I saw cinder block rubble, razor wire and rebar. Processing the experience was akin to trying to make sense of the Revelation writer's end-time apocalyptic narrative.

It is tempting to foster a consuming contempt for an obviously corrupt Haitian government, considering billions of charitably donated dollars have flowed in over the years. What saves me from stumbling into a morass of disdain, woe and sorrow each time I go to this Caribbean island is the spirit of the people we serve there. These Christ-led folk are oblivious to their tribulations. They do not know what "third world" means. They believe! Faith nurtures self-worth in their day-to-day, purpose-driven lives. To quote the prophet Isaiah, a key source of writer John's inspiration, *"Therefore with joy, you will draw water from the wells of salvation"* (Isaiah 12:3). These Haitians' joy was our mission team's salvation!

Oh, Good Shepherd, may the tears You wipe from our eyes be of joy only. Amen.

Festival Day–Discernment

Do you know what the red flags are for you? What habits or proclivities (false idols) will take you off course or away from God's will? What methods can you employ to head back into the good and perfect will of our Father?

When was the last time your desire for control turned against you? Cite a time when you decided to let go and let God. What were the results?

During this 40-day devotional study, have you had difficulty staying with your fast? What tries your patience the most throughout the day and tempts you to abandon spiritual focus?

Have you held hands in church lately? When last did you hold hands while praying with someone, or a small group?

When did you witness an expression of love in a nonverbal fashion this past week?

Make a point to watch a good tearjerker movie soon. Do it as a small group. Don't forget to take a box of Kleenex!

Chapter III

COMPLETION

THE FINAL WEEK OF THIS 40-DAY JOURNEY
will bring us out of the material senses and into our
spiritual sixth sense, where we experience our call from the
Father through the Holy Spirit. If you are reading this as
part of a Lenten study, this 40-day journey will bring us to
Holy Week. The story of Christ comes full circle with His
resurrection and paves the way for the arrival of the Holy
Spirit as captured in Luke's story of the Emmaus road disciples (see Luke 24) and the Acts of the apostles.

Prayer to the Holy Spirit

Come, Holy Spirit
Fill the hearts of Your faithful and
Kindle in us the fire of Your Love.
Send forth Your Spirit and
we shall be recreated, and
You shall renew the face of the earth.
Oh God Who, by the light of the Holy Spirit,
did instruct the hearts of the faithful,
grant that by that same Holy Spirit
we may be truly wise and
ever enjoy Your consolations.
Through Christ our Lord.
Amen.

DIMENSIONS OF LOVE

*I pray that out of his glorious riches he may strengthen you
with power through his Spirit in your inner being, so that
Christ may dwell in your hearts through faith. And I pray
that you, being rooted and established in love, may have
power, together with all the Lord's holy people, to grasp how
wide and long and high and deep is the love of Christ, and
to know this love that surpasses knowledge—that you may
be filled to the measure of all the fullness of God.*
– Ephesians 3:16-19

THE FIRST SIGN WAS HEARING MY WIFE'S morning sickness coming from our bathroom instead of the hum of a hair dryer. It was a love sign, one of many that would play out over the next few months. This was a desired for, hard-fought pregnancy, including pre-conception invasive surgery for the father. Over the course of that journey into fatherhood, I learned firsthand what the mother experiences leading up to childbirth. The bond that occurs between mother and child during pregnancy is a proportion of love that cannot be measured. It is inestimable by the dimensions of this world.

I have seen it, not only in the mother of my two daughters, but also in the eyes of pregnant women everywhere. While the fetus is draining them of vital nutrients — a new life's sustenance — causing nausea and newly-developed dental cavities, the look in these women's eyes remains peaceful. Contented, they gently and lovingly rub their tummies. God strengthens these mothers through His powerful Spirit to the core of their inner being. It is why I believe that many young and new parents gravitate back to the Church. Certainly, it is a divine reattraction, born from a spiritual post-partum separation. The entire experience of bringing one of these little ones into the world connects the parents to the Father. Much of the time, Mom and Dad are not even aware of this link of love to Abba. It is the unmerited love immersed in His prevenient grace that connects with the divine pilot light of their souls.

Humankind is descendent from the Creator. We are His progeny. It is through the glorious riches of our offspring that we discover love's roots and firmly establish ourselves in His righteousness. The door opens in our hearts, inviting Christ to come dwell with us. Then we may further know the extent of His love and be *"filled to the measure of all the fullness of God."*

Abba, we long for the day when the world will universally recognize Your sanctification of each unborn child. May it be so! Amen.

COME, GENTLE GUIDE

The wind blows wherever it pleases. You hear its sound, but
you cannot tell where it comes from or where it is going. So it
is with everyone born of the Spirit.
— John 3:8

GROWING UP IN MIAMI, FLORIDA, I CHER-
ished the ever-present touch of a Biscayne Bay breeze
tossing my hair. The recognizable smell of salt air often
goes unnoticed until you find yourself living in a land-
locked locale far from the coast. Regularly, the wind blows
inshore from the ocean, steady and constant. To a surfer
boy's delight, it would sometimes blow offshore, creating
well-formed breakers. Hurricane season brings the specter
of violent and destructive high winds. Standing outdoors
in the eye of the storm one will experience absolute stillness,
where there is no flicker of a match flame. This quiet place
is the quintessential calm before the storm. Going out of
the eye, away from the center of the storm, puts one at the
mercy of the most intense winds of a hurricane.

The breath of the Holy Spirit is a gentle guide when it
comes from me, inside out, softly leading a pen across the
page or choreographing fingertips as they dance across a
keyboard. The same Spirit comes from the outside, rolling
in on emotional waves, inducing goose bump ripples across
the flesh. Spirit soars in on the majestic wings of Abba's
unmerited love and greets me with the sweet, fresh, rustling

sound of a swaying pine forest. Caught up in free-flowing waves of grace, tears flow freely from this writer. I know I am experiencing His generously offered, justifying grace. I have not earned this unmerited love.

When I was seven years old, I heard the wind blow in a new manner. It was not the familiar fury of the common hurricane, but the atypical howl of a locomotive. The rare Miami tornado went right over our house, tearing off part of the roof. That night, our family rushed to huddle in the home's center living room. A big, beautifully fat sabal palm tree growing out front saved us from a scythe-like threshing. The next morning, the family gazed in wonder out a shattered, big bay window. A twelve-foot band of frame aluminum, snatched up from the screened-in pool across the street, was wrapped around our sabal palm like a trash bag twist tie. A broad and sturdy tree allowed us to live another day, born of the Spirit.

Come, Holy Spirit, surround our senses with the saving grace of the precious Son. Amen.

UNSEEN ACCEPTANCE

Therefore we do not lose heart. Though outwardly we are
wasting away, yet inwardly we are being renewed day by
day. For our light and momentary troubles are achieving for
us an eternal glory that far outweighs them all. So we fix
our eyes not on what is seen, but on what is unseen, since
what is seen is temporary, but what is unseen is eternal.
– 2 Corinthians 4:16-18

I WANT TO BELIEVE I HAVE ALWAYS HAD A BIG heart. In fact, I believe we all start out with big hearts. We can see it in the wide-eyed, joyful innocence of our children, for they see the Kingdom of God. Jesus told us we can enter the Kingdom through the eyes of children (see Mark 10:15). We receive the Kingdom by our wholehearted, innocent acceptance of His abundant grace and mercy, offered in each eternally present moment. Somewhere in the transition from adolescence to adulthood, many of us lose heart. It has happened with me more than once. With innocence evaporating, I became hard-hearted, same as losing heart. I had begun the turning away, looking down instead of looking up. Losing heart and losing faith is akin to the chicken and the egg.

At the age of fifty-six, I had lost heart. I found myself handcuffed in the back of a Georgia State Patrol car. My reliance on the bottle to find a momentary peace backfired for the last time. Even in the misery and humiliation of that situation, God grabbed my attention. On the way to jail, I looked up. As I gazed through a metal cage, I could see a nametag on the dash: "*Officer Harrold*". My father was named Harold. It is not a common name and, in that instant, there was a moment of childhood presence. I have never taken that moment for granted! After I bonded out of jail, a cab driver hearing my story would remark, "You should be thankful you did not have an accident and kill someone." In another eternal moment, God again slapped me upside the head!

I quit drinking and got sober because of that experience, finding my heart again. My momentary troubles have achieved for me a turning that placed me firmly in the arms of a merciful Father. I do not believe in coincidences anymore. As a friend suggested to me once, those little instances are just God winking at you. With that wink He says to me, "It's okay, just hold My hand. Stay with Me." I've grown older and my body is withering away, but my spirit is being renewed day by day in relationship with my unseen Creator.

Father, we long to be the child innocently accepting the wonder of Your eternal love and mercy as we once again enter Your Kingdom. Amen.

LAST WORDS

And I will ask the Father, and he will give you another
advocate to help you and be with you forever— the Spirit of
truth. The world cannot accept him because it neither sees
him nor knows him. But you know him, for he lives with
you and will be in you.
− John 14:16-17

T HE MOST TRAUMATIC AND SHOCKINGLY
sad moments in this life we share are centered around
the death of loved ones. The experience shakes us to our
bones, and we question what is true in this existence of ours.
In the final analysis, we must rely on our conclusion of faith
based on non-empirical evidence. To the world, this evidence is literally nonsense. Today's scripture passage comes
from what is commonly referred to as Jesus' final or farewell
discourse with His disciples. He has already washed their
feet and broken bread with them for the last time. He is
teaching all the way to the very end.

One of my reoccurring questions about life has been
to wonder which is more emotionally painful, the loss of a
beloved from a long illness or an unexpected, sudden death?
The experience of separation by death has no variance in
degree of difficulty. There is possibly one differential. With
greater warning approaching a death, one may have the
opportunity for final words with their dearest. When I was
twelve years old, the phone rang in our house one day and I

picked up the upstairs phone simultaneously with my aunt Betty, who answered in our kitchen downstairs. Listening to the conversation, I learned of my father's sudden death by heart failure. Thirty years later, I would answer a different phone and hear my brother Hal speak of our mother dying in a car accident. Over the years, a variation of the same question always arises in me, "What would I say if I had a chance at one last conversation with Mom and Dad?"

Christ truthfully tells us in these verses from John, that we will always have the opportunity for last words. Through the Spirit of Truth, aka Holy Spirit, our Heavenly Father provides another (translated variously) *Helper, Advocate, Counselor,* and *Comforter* to facilitate what the world calls "closure". However, in the believer's realm, it is not closure but a liberating opening of a new and graceful door. Now we find ourselves in a place where we know our beloved dwell with and in us forever.

Abba, we long for the blessed assurance that another Comforter is always with us and there are no last words, forever. Amen.

ETERNAL DIVIDENDS

We know that the whole creation has been groaning as in the pains of childbirth right up to the present time. Not only so, but we ourselves, who have the firstfruits of the Spirit, groan inwardly as we wait eagerly for our adoption to sonship, the redemption of our bodies. For in this hope we were saved. But hope that is seen is no hope at all. Who hopes for what they already have? But if we hope for what we do not yet have, we wait for it patiently.
– Romans 8:22-25

I LONG SO TO GET *IT* RIGHT; I HAVE BEEN struggling my entire life to get *it* right. Only now am I seeking to define, clarify, understand what exactly *it* is. What is *it*? Our society would define *it* as success, winning in competition, recognition, celebrity. *It* is a trophy cabinet filled to the brim: wife, car, house and children. Over my lifetime, my culture has succeeded in convincing me *it* is everything that is ephemeral and temporal. I am groaning because I am never full, never fulfilled. Yet, I strain to convince myself otherwise with vain delusions. These days, *it* is coming into focus and defined by the prescient facets of salvation, atonement and wholeness. Now my hope is in what is not seen: firstfruits of the Spirit, a divine, flickering pilot light within.

I have worked in various professions and industries throughout my life. The meandering list reads: television cameraman/reporter, marketing/public relations director, financial consultant, bartender, restaurant manager, district sales manager and motorcycle salesman. For forty years, I hoped for a paycheck and measured myself by the balance in my bank account. No matter how big the number, it was no hope at all. Recently, it occurred to me that I have always been paid in another better way. Customers, coworkers, suppliers, the friends I have met and established relationships with, the bonds we formed with fondness and admiration the Spirit fosters; these experiences are a divine reward, enriching me with eternal dividends.

Each new day, I get a little closer to Yahweh. As my faith walk grows, evermore abiding in Christ and Christ in me, I take less and less for granted. I believe Abba places people in our path for a reason, just as He places us in the others' paths. There is no need to define the reason, for it will be revealed in His time. We were meant to be in fellowship where two or more are gathered (see Matthew 18:20). *It* is cumulative, each new instance adding another brick in the wall of our adoption into the sonship, for which we wait eagerly. *It* is in this hope through which I am saved.

Father, may we all wait eagerly for the day when, adopted, we will share in Your house the many mansions of the sonship. Amen.

THE ORDER OF THINGS

Then I saw "a new heaven and a new earth," for the first heaven and the first earth had passed away, and there was no longer any sea. I saw the Holy City, the new Jerusalem, coming down out of heaven from God, prepared as a bride beautifully dressed for her husband. And I heard a loud voice from the throne saying, "Look! God's dwelling place is now among the people, and he will dwell with them. They will be his people, and God himself will be with them and be their God. 'He will wipe every tear from their eyes. There will be no more death' or mourning or crying or pain, for the old order of things has passed away."

He who was seated on the throne said, "I am making everything new!" Then he said, "Write this down, for these words are trustworthy and true."

He said to me: "It is done. I am the Alpha and the Omega, the Beginning and the End. To the thirsty I will give water without cost from the spring of the water of life. Those who are victorious will inherit all this, and I will be their God and they will be my children.

– Revelation 21:1-7

OLD HABITS ARE HARD TO BREAK. THEY are the substance and stability of our world's comfort zones. They are the dog at my feet, the morning paper on the front door stoop, a cold beer in hand watching my home team, my favorite fishing hole, my self-designated pew at church on Sunday. All these things contribute to and, in fact, are the order of my life. This order, in its predictable sequence at its appointed time, gives me the cozy illusion that I am in control. Yes, I am pleasantly moored in my very neatly-designed, snug harbor.

A few years back, I was caught up in a very accelerated period of spiritual growth. I had an almost insatiable hunger to get closer to my Creator. This desire for a more intimate relationship with Abba was the result of a humbling life event. On my recovery road, I accepted an invitation to be a pilgrim on a three-day, Christ-focused men's cloistered retreat. Over two dozen of us had to give up our cell phones, watches and any means of contact with our outside world. About two days into the weekend, I began to lose the unneeded, time-bound, worldly habit burdens. I literally shed the "old order of things" (v.4) that only clouded my inner vision. My expectation became only to witness the presence of Yahweh.

Each pilgrim, as part of their completion of the program, gave a short summation at the end about what the retreat had meant to them. Mine was of revelation. I experienced what Jesus was talking about on the mount that day when He prayed, *"on earth as it is in heaven."* Our home for the weekend (the King's Retreat, as the facility is named) was most certainly holy ground, a new Jerusalem, God's dwelling place. There also with us, was a great cloud of witnesses bringing the agape that wipes away all tears. I have been back there many times since in a servant's role, and always the freely flowing Spirit is food for the angels!

Father, may we always remember Your dwelling place with us is within Your trustworthy and true, never-ending love. Amen.

Festival Day–Discernment

Read Luke 18:15-16, meditate and pray on its meaning for you.

Make time each day to be still outside. Eagerly await the sound in the wind, the breath of the Holy Spirit.

When you taste a bite of Angel Food Cake, receive it with innocent acceptance. Be sure to wink back at Abba.

Write a note of forever words to a beloved who has passed on.

Who is one you have met in your work life who is invaluable to you? Remind them how much they mean to you!

Make plans to go on a cloistered retreat with like-minded people of faith some time in the next year.

Use an angel food cake recipe and bake a cake (or cakes) to enjoy together in fellowship with your family, Sunday school class or study group. Here is one to try:

Rebecca Coltrin Bosworth Angel Food Cake Recipe

T HE BEAUTIFUL MOTHER OF OUR TWO PRE-
cious daughters, Margaret Elizabeth and Jeanne Faye,
contributes this Southern Illinois recipe that has roots in
the Sewell family tree. Becky is a proud Yankee, born and
raised in a Chicago suburb. However, her roots are steeped
in the southern influences of Cave-In-Rock, Illinois, across
the Ohio River from Kentucky.

Becky describes her recipe thusly: "*The advantage of
growing up with women of Southern descent is their knowledge of baking. Angel food cake was always the birthday cake
in the family, any time of year. It always appeared to be made
effortlessly. Looking back now as an adult and knowing there
was no air-conditioning, convection ovens or egg separators, I
have an appreciation for the love and effort that went into that
cake, especially having failed two of three times attempting to
make one. The cake that did 'make it' was delicious, beautiful
and made me feel like a child again.*"

1 ½ cups egg whites (12-13 eggs)
1 ¼ teaspoon cream of tartar
½ teaspoon salt
1 ¾ cup Grace Sugar Measure Lily
1 ¼ teaspoon Flavoring 1 cup + 2 tablespoons flour

Beat egg whites with wire whip. Add cream of tartar, salt
when eggs are frothy, continue beating until the point of
egg whites stands upright. Gradually beat in one cup sugar
which has been sifted twice. Fold in flavoring. Sift flour

once before measuring. Fold in flour gradually after sifting three times with the remaining ¾ cups of sugar, pour into ungreased 10" tube pan and bake 65 minutes, in mid -oven at 325 degrees. Invert pan (flip upside/down) until cake is completely cooled.

<u>White Boiled Icing</u>:
½ cup sugar
¼ cup white syrup

Beat together till it threads

Beat 2 sm egg whites till stiff and add sugar mixture.
1 Teaspoon Vanilla Say *Amen!*

Chapter IV

AFTER WORDS

I AM HUMBLED AND IMMENSELY BLESSED YOU have picked up and opened this book. Perhaps you have read it and participated in the 40-day fast. It is possible that you have opened it for the first time to this spot in the back of the book. I've done it often with various books myself. No problem; sometimes eating desert first is a real joy. Keep on reading and praying. You're an angel, thank you!

ICING ON THE CAKE

*Do not neglect to show hospitality to strangers, for by doing
that some have entertained angels without knowing it.*
– Hebrews 13:2 (NRSV)

I SHUDDER TO THINK WHERE MY LIFE WOULD be in this world without the angels who have graced my path. You have read of a few in this book. One I have mentioned is Aunt Betty, my godmother and my mother's aunt, whom Jeanne knew as a sister. Aunt Betty was the person who cared for me as a little boy when my parents were traveling, which was often. She took that little boy fishing for the very first time and held him, crying, in her arms after his pee-wee football team lost a cold, November-league championship game. She left this life in her prime after suffering a fatal brain aneurism when that same boy was barely thirteen years of age. A framed visage of her has graced his nightstand throughout the years.

Angels are prominent and play pivotal roles in the story of God. The title of this book comes from an angel's rescuing encouragement of the prophet Elijah (1 Kings 19). Fresh from His baptism encounter with the Holy Spirit and exhausted by the pesky temptations of the devil in the wilderness, Jesus was attended to by the angels (Matthew 4). The divine plan of redemption for humanity comes full circle when angels bring a Jew (Peter) and Gentile (Cornelius) together, facilitating the spread of the Gospel throughout the new world (Acts 10). When we are willing to welcome strangers as Cornelius did with Peter, wonderful, life-changing miracles can occur.

I once I worked at a local Harley-Davidson dealership, and this employment required me to work most Sundays. I began attending our church's 8:30am worship service before reporting to work. In the pew in front of me, there was a regular group of church ladies. I had developed an admiration for them as I saw and exchanged pleasantries with them on Sunday mornings. Many times, I would ride my Harley to this worship service, riding gear and all. One Sunday after the service, one of the ladies mentioned to me that she had it on her bucket list to ride on the back of a motorcycle! Her name was Betty. I had surmised that she was old enough to be my mother/aunt. Betty's bucket list declaration grabbed my attention, touched my heart and planted a seed that would remain in my consciousness for months to come.

A year passed as I struggled with how to prudently facilitate the fulfillment of Betty's aspiration. Then my position at work transitioned and I found myself working in our rentals department. This move turned out to be providential. In the rental fleet, there was a model known as a "Tri-Glide," a three-wheeler which possessed a stability characteristic that gave me confidence we could safely help Betty accomplish her goal. On a late October Sunday, I asked her if she was ready to take her ride. Without hesitation and beaming, she nodded yes!

A few days before the November ride, her son brought her into the dealership for orientation. Since she was in her 80's, I was concerned about Betty's stamina. She practiced getting on and off the trike and tried on helmets. I encouraged her to take one home to wear around the house some and get used to its weight. I will forever have this joyfully tender image in my heart of her: helmet on, contentedly walking around her home the days and nights before our ride.

The experience with my church lady friend was chock full of graceful moments. In my heart there was a nearness, a presence of the love I knew from my Aunt Betty, and my mom, Jeanne. In and through the entire process there were God moments, miracles that earlier in my life I might have labeled coincidences. While we were filling out the necessary paperwork at the dealership, I shared with Betty and her son my ideas about the route we would take on the ride. I knew that fatigue could be an issue for Betty, so I suggested a short route that would take us by Patak Meats, a favorite butcher shop at which I was hoping to stop and shop. She and her son paused and looked at each other. Gracing me with a big smile and beaming once more, Betty explained that her grandson Dakota worked there. It was a wonderfully graceful experience taking my friend Betty for her first motorcycle ride. Later, while I shopped for sausages and steaks, Betty exchanged her motorcycle helmet for a hardhat and received a VIP tour of the factory from her grandson.

Abba, may we always be willing to take nothing for granted, so we might enjoy the miracle of Your creation, our small world. Amen.

P.S., I Love You

YAHWEH ALWAYS HAS ONE MORE POSTSCRIPT miracle for each of us in all our life's struggles and triumphs. He sends us afterthought signs, as though he is winking at us. He is saying, "P.S., I love you!"

Applying the finishing touches to *Angel Food Cake* were difficult for this writer. It was almost as if I did not really want to say goodbye to the effort. I was uncertain if the "Angels" theme for my final words was the best way to go. Then arrived one evening in July — approximately three years after starting the project — while I was watching my beloved Atlanta Braves. I saw a news report about the Los Angeles Angels' tribute to their young pitcher, Tyler Skaggs, whose sudden death had sent shockwaves through Major League Baseball. At their first home game after his passing, the team held a memorial tribute to Skaggs, who also happened to be a native southern Californian. The aggregate love flowing through the stadium permeated throughout the ceremony to the point that miracles began to occur in so many ways. His mom, Debbie, threw out the first pitch. It was a strike right down the center of the plate! Tyler Skaggs' colleagues on the Angels' pitching staff threw a combined no-hitter against the Seattle Mariners. It was the Angels' first combined no-hitter since July 13, 1991, which also happened to be the day Tyler Skaggs was born into this world. It was the 11th no-hitter in the Angels franchise's history – the same number Skaggs wore at Santa Monica High School. On the eve of what would have been Tyler's twenty-eighth birthday (7/13/19), the LA Angels began their no-hit victory by scoring seven runs in the first inning, getting thirteen hits overall and winning 13-0. Abba, with Tyler Skaggs by His side, was winking at us all. Take nothing for granted. There are no coincidences; only God's little miracles.

Love always and in all ways,
Brad xxoo

Scripture Index

All AFC Scripture Listings are NIV translation unless otherwise noted.

Introduction: Genesis 7:4; Exodus 24:18; Deuteronomy 10:4; 1 Kings 19:4-9 NKJV; Matthew 4:2

Eschewal: Titus 2:11-12

Chapter 1 Beginnings-First Steps: I Peter 2:2; Habakkuk 2:1-3; Matthew 18:20; Deuteronomy 28:2; Luke 6:41; 2 Corinthians 2:14-15; Psalm 34; Mark 7:20-22; John 8:31-32

Chapter 2 Transition:

Taste: 1 Corinthians 15:34; Matthew 5:13; Psalm 119:103; 1 Peter 2:2-3; Hebrews 6:4-6; Mark 14:36; Ezekiel 3:3; Song of Songs 4:9-16

Smell: Job 39:25; James 5:16, KJV; Luke 7:37-38; Song of Songs 4:9-10; Genesis 2.24; Matthew 2:11; Exodus 30:34; Revelation 18:13; Proverbs 27:9; John 15:13; Revelation 8:1-4, NKJV;

See: 2 Corinthians 4:16-18; Exodus 33:13, NKJV; Luke 9:62; Matthew 6:34; Mark 8:24-25; Ecclesiastes 7:15, NKJV; Ecclesiastes 3:1-8; John 1:45-48; John 14:6

Hear: Jonah 3:1-5; Luke 8:17; James 3:5; Colossians 4:6; Matthew 11:28; Psalm 18:6; 2 Timothy 1:13-14; Matthew 18:20

Touch: Jeremiah 18:1-6; Matthew 18:20; Genesis 32:24-30; Exodus 32:1-4; Isaiah 41:13; 1 John: 4:16; 1 John 1:1; Revelation 7:13-17; Isaiah 12:2

Chapter 3 Release-Completion

Insight/Intuition: Ephesians 3:16-19; John 3:8; 2 Corinthians 4:16-18; Mark 10:15; John 14:16-17; Romans 8:22-25; Matthew 18:20; Revelation 21:1-7; Luke 18:15-16.

After Words

Icing on the Cake: Hebrews 13:2

BIBLIOGRAPHY

The Anonymous Press Study Edition of Alcoholics Anonymous, 11th printing 2008, Anonymouse Press, http:// anonpress.org

Beck, Glenn, *The Immortal Nicholas; A novel*, New York: Mercury Radio Art and Simon & Schuster, 2015, https://www.simonandschuster.com/books/ The-Immortal-Nicholas/Glenn-Beck/9781476798844

Fee, Gordon Fee, and Douglas Stewart, *How to Read the Bible Book by Book: a guided tour*. New York: Zondervan/Harper Collins Publishing, 2002.

Lewis, C.S., quote – "A woman's heart," *GoodReads,* Accessed August 6, 2021, https://www.goodreads. com/quotes/346839;

Maxwell, John C., and Nelson Bibles Staff, *The Maxwell Leadership Bible*, 2nd ed. (New York: Thomas Nelson/ Harper Collins Publishing, 2007), 987.

Merriam-Webster Dictionary Online, s.v. "include," accessed August 6, 2021, https://www.merriam-webster.com/ thesaurus/include.

Merriam-Webster Dictionary Online, s.v. "reveille," accessed August 6, 2021, https://www.merriam-webster.com/ dictionary/reveille.

Merriam-Webster Dictionary Online, s.v. "syzygy," accessed August 6, 2021, https://www.merriam-webster.com/dictionary/syzygy.

Reagan, Will and United Pursuit, "Set a Fire," *Live at the Banks House,* Set a Fire Lyrics on Genius. Accessed August 6, 2021. https://genius.com/Will-reagan-and-united-pursuit-set-a-fire-lyrics

CPSIA information can be obtained
at www.ICGtesting.com
Printed in the USA
BVHW071839111121
621211BV00004B/554

9 781662 828553